Lawns

LAWNS

Series Concept: Robert J. Dolezal
Encyclopedia Concept: Barbara K. Dolezal
Managing Editor: Louise Damberg
Copy Editors: Nancy Strege, Kathy Talley-Jones
Photography Editor: John M. Rickard
Designer: Jerry Simon
Layout Artists: Rik Boyd, Andrea Reider
Photoshop Artist: Ryan Pressler
Horticulturists: Carrie Heinley, Peggy Henry, Kathy Talley-Jones
Photo Stylists: Joyce M. Almstad, Carrie Heinley, Peggy Henry
Research: Dave Bullis, Shelley Ring Diamond
Index: Rick Hurd

Copyright © 2000
Creative Publishing international, Inc.
5900 Green Oak Drive
Minnetonka, MN 55343
1-800-328-3895
All rights reserved
Printed in U.S.A. by World Color Press
10 9 8 7 6 5 4 3 2 1

President/CEO: David D. Murphy
Vice President/Editorial: Patricia K. Jacobsen
Vice President/Retail Sales & Marketing: Richard M. Miller

Home Improvement/*Gardening*
Executive Editor: Bryan Trandem
Editorial Director: Jerri Farris
Creative Director: Tim Himsel

Created by: Dolezal & Associates,
in partnership with Creative Publishing international, Inc.,
in cooperation with Black & Decker.
 BLACK&DECKER is a trademark of the Black & Decker
Corporation and is used under license.

Library of Congress
Cataloging-in-Publication Data

(Information on file)

ISBN 0–86573–439–9 (hardcover)
ISBN 0–86573–444–5 (softcover)

PHOTOGRAPHY & ILLUSTRATION

PRINCIPAL PHOTOGRAPHY

JOHN RICKARD: Cover and pgs. *iv* (top, 3rd from top, and bot), *v* (top, 3rd from top, and bot), *vi, vii, viii,* 3, 4, 5, 6, 7, 10, 16, 17, 19 (top), 20, 21, 22 (top), 28 (bot), 31, 33, 38, 41, 43 (steps 4–5), 46, 47, 52, 53, 56 (mid & bot), 60 (bot), 61, 62, 64 (top), 65, 66 (L), 72, 73, 74, 77, 78 (bot), 79, 80, 82 (bot), 84, 85, 97 (top)

OTHER PHOTOGRAPHY

TIM BUTLER: pgs. *iv* (2nd from top), 13 (top), 34, 64 (steps 1–3), 70, 71, 95 (bot), 96, 97 (bot), 98 (bot), 99 (top), 101 (top)

KYLE CHESSER: pgs. 22 (bot), 23, 26, 28 (top), 40, 76, 78 (top)

DOUG DEALEY: pg. 8 (top L & bot)

ROBERT DOLEZAL: pg. 35 (steps 2–3)

REED ESTABROOK: pgs. *iv* (2nd from top), 2, 9 (top), 12, 13 (bot), 14 (bot), 15 (bot), 24, 27, 29, 42, 43 (steps 2–3), 44, 45, 48, 49, 50, 51, 58 (bot), 59 (bot step 4)

DAVID GOLDBERG: pgs. 14 (top), 58 (top), 59 (bot steps 2–3), 66 (bot R), 67 (steps 1, 3, 4), 68, 69

SAXON HOLT: pg. 99 (bot)

IMAGEPOINT: pgs. 30, 32, 35 (steps 1 & 4), 36, 37, 54, 56 (top), 57, 59 (top steps 1–3), 67 (step 2), 81, 82 (top), 88, 89, 90, 91, 92, 93, 95 (top)

CHARLES NUCCI: pgs. 18, 19 (bot), 94, 98 (top), 100, 101 (bot)

PAM PEIRCE: pg. 60 (top)

CHARLES SLAY: pgs. 8 (top R), 9 (bot), 83

ILLUSTRATION: RON HILDEBRAND

LAWNS

Author
Carol A. Crotta

Photographer
John M. Rickard

Series Concept
Robert J. Dolezal

CREATIVE
PUBLISHING
international

Minnetonka, Minnesota

CONTENTS

PLANTING
A NEW LAWN

Page 39

RENOVATING
AN EXISTING LAWN

Page 55

RESTORING
YOUR LAWN

Page 63

BASIC LAWN CARE

Page 75

TURFGRASSES &
GROUNDCOVERS

Page 87

INTRODUCTION

For many of us, the image of a home surrounded by a velvety green lawn is as close to domestic bliss as it comes. It's easy to understand why.

Grass is a feel-good thing. Just the sounds of mowing and the scent of fresh-mown grass can send us into childhood reverie. A lawn also is a great facilitator. It gives structure to yards and boundaries to flower beds. Kids frolic on it and when they fall, there's no cause for worry, because a good lawn is a soft cushion. We host parties, play catch with the dog, and sun

> *It may be argued further that real beauty is neither in garden nor landscape, but in the relation of both to the individual, that what we are seeing is not only a scenic setting for pool and fountain and parterre, but a background for life.*
>
> Sir George Sitwell

ourselves on it. There simply is no substitute for the incomparable beauty, tranquillity, and function of a great lawn.

Groundcovers—low-growing plants that spread across the ground—create the same expanse of serenity as grass and require less maintenance, making them a perfect choice for those too busy to devote much time to yard work. More and more, people with less and less time are opting to plant low-growing, and often fragrant, groundcovers, some of which can even stand the stress test of turfgrass.

You might imagine that perfection in a lawn or groundcover is a tough goal for the home gardener. Planted properly, a near-perfect lawn requires less maintenance than you may

think, and groundcover, once established, even less work. Helping you to achieve that goal is precisely the purpose of this book.

In these pages, you will learn how to evaluate your existing lawn, renovate it, or replace it with seed, sod, or plugs of grass, or with groundcover perfectly suited to your climate and needs. You also will learn the proper way to maintain a lawn to avoid having to replace or renovate it, at least in the near future.

You may decide, after reading this book, to hire a professional to work on your lawn for you. Either way, you will at least have gained an understanding of, and perhaps newfound appreciation for, the grass—or groundcover—beneath your feet. Enjoy the journey.

F

or every garden site and situation, there is a turfgrass or groundcover suited to it. No yard is too small, nor too big, to support a lawn.

If your summers are hot and steamy, or hot and dry, or cool and wet, there are lawns that will perform for you. If you live in an apartment in a dense urban area and garden on the roof, there are lawns that will prosper in raised beds or containers. If your yard is a constant whirlwind of children, pets, and their toys, there are lawns that can withstand the punishment. If your one true desire in life is to re-create the serene Korea grass, moss, and azalea garden you saw on your last visit to a botanical garden, you can have that, too. The effects of a soothing green expanse are not limited to turfgrass, either; there are groundcovers that can provide the same feeling with greater texture and diversity.

In the following pages, we spotlight just a few of the choices, from functional to purely fun, and engage you to imagine others. While lawns often are regarded as the ultimate utility planting in a yard—taken for granted as backdrops to flowers and trees—that view is changing. Grasses and groundcovers as decorative plants have come into their own. Landscape designers are giving them their due, planting them alone in urns and vases, allowing them to "drip" over the edges of dry fountains, creating rooftop sculptural troughs of tall grasses that can be viewed through clerestory windows.

As you take in the images on the following pages, let your mind wander through the countless possibilities that would add that special something to your own landscape and garden.

> Lawns have evolved from the purely functional to the downright decorative— and everything in between

Beautiful Lawns and Groundcovers

A well-tended house surrounded by a picket fence and manicured lawn is a quintessential domestic portrait. Lawn care is a passion and a hobby for many, with a velvety-smooth green lawn free of weeds and brown patches a most satisfying reward.

SMALL-SPACE LAWNS

Many of us tend to think of lawns as sweeping pools of green that dominate the suburban yard. In most cities, however, the only place you'll see a large lawn is in a park or on civic or museum grounds. Small-space lawns truly can be special. In the confines of a small apartment garden, townhouse courtyard, or small city garden, a well-placed, well-manicured lawn planting can be an exceptional design element.

With small-space lawns, it's best to think of them more as planting beds, like flower beds. The trick is to keep the turf in scale. Avoid situations where the lawn is small but surrounded by very large trees or huge shrubs, for the garden will seem poorly proportioned. Think small scale for the yard as a whole and opt for dwarf trees and shrubs that can be controlled easily in height and spread. Japanese-garden design theories, which are masterful in keeping a garden in proportion, might provide good supplemental reading and be a source of ideas.

One of the most attractive designs for a small-space lawn is a central, geometrically shaped lawn bed surrounded by a brick or stone walkway lined with flower borders. You can set a pillar, large urn, birdbath, statue, small fountain, or other sculptural piece at the far end of the lawn area to serve as a focal point. Perhaps you would prefer the focus to be a beautiful, small-specimen tree, such as an elegant Japanese dwarf maple (*Acer palmatum*). You might consider installing a bench, a couple of Adirondack chairs, or a bistro table and chairs. Whatever you do, a small lawn can be a jewel of brilliant green within a setting of more colorful, textured plantings.

Small-space lawns can be grown from any turfgrass that is adapted to your climate. If your garden receives less than half a day of shade or there is no direct sun at all, choose a turfgrass that is shade tolerant. If light permits, groundcovers such as Irish moss or dichondra also make a beautiful small-space statement.

A small garden area can still support a lawn. The key is to keep the lawn and surrounding plantings in proportion to one another. A small-space lawn often benefits from a focal point, such as a beautiful specimen bush or dwarf tree, a decorative bench or sculpture.

CONTAINER LAWNS

Lawns are scarce in the city, probably because many people think the typical city apartment is an unlikely place for a lawn to grow. Lawns, however, are supremely adaptable, and with clever planning, they can adapt to the urban environment, especially when they are treated as a decorative element.

One simple way you can install a "lawn" on your apartment balcony is to have a bit of fun and plant one in a terra-cotta pot or other container the way you would annuals or a flowering vine. Turfgrass will grow in pots if you match a loose potting soil to a well-draining pot. Fill the container close to the rim and water the potting mix well; add more potting soil if necessary to establish the proper soil depth. Then, simply seed a grass variety that's good for your climate zone, topcoat it with a scattering of mulch, water it in, and watch it grow.

It's likely you'll need to choose a seed mix designed for shade, since city balconies often offer open shade. You'll also need to water more frequently than you would a lawn planted in open ground since pots tend to be porous, causing the soil in them to dry out quickly. Let the turfgrass grow to a desired length, then clip it with hand shears to keep it trimmed and neat. Fertilize with one-quarter-strength liquid fertilizer every two weeks, when you water.

Several pots of turfgrass intermingled with containers of colorful annuals can create a charming, cheery look. Another great look is to plant spring or summer bulbs with the lawn to create a mini-meadow. Dichondra and some mosses also make a wonderful container groundcover look to mix in with your other pots.

If you have access to a rooftop or a small, terraced courtyard or patio, you can grow lawn in a raised bed. Colonial bent grass—the preferred grass for putting greens—and some of the fescues, particularly hard fescue, grow quite well in a raised bed, but any grass suited to your area will grow if the soil is prepared properly. Once you have fashioned your raised bed, start with a potting mix that drains well and top it with an inch (25 mm) of playground sand to support the turfgrass rhizomes. Topcoat the seeds and water in. As with containers, you need to water more frequently (depending on rainfall amounts), fertilize at quarter- to half-strength, and keep the lawn neat by clipping with shears.

Lawns are turning up in the most unusual–and creative–places these days. Try planting a lawn in a broad-topped container to create a playful homage to the classic dream home. Here, grasslike Scotch moss doubles as turfgrass.

EXPANSIVE LAWNS

If you live in Canada, the Midwest, the Northeast, or the Atlantic South, you well know the big-lawn look. Housing tracts can run to an acre, with no division between properties. In some areas, local ordinances prohibit fencing or shrub lines that divide one house from another. As a result, lawns are expansive, with each house set centrally in a framework of small trees, shrubs, and flower beds.

If your lawn is large and covers most of the property, you may lack time to coddle and coo over every corner of it. Even if you did have the time, you probably would prefer to spare the resources or budget required for a demanding turfgrass. You likely ride a small tractor mower to get the trimming job done and rely mainly on rainwater to keep the lawn nourished.

For a lawn this size, you need a hardy turfgrass that is thick, slow growing, and durable. You'll also want a grass that can adapt to some shade if you have large trees on the property. Fescues for northern climates and St. Augustine grass, Bahia grass, and hybrid Bermuda grass in southern turfgrass areas are solid choices for the big lawn.

Tearing out an existing expansive lawn to install a new lawn from scratch is difficult and impractical. However, you can "overturf," or overseed, your existing lawn—in essence, create a second lawn on top of the existing lawn—with one that will look and perform better, relying on the new seed to crowd out the old.

Begin by eliminating weeds and laying down an inch (25 mm) of fresh topsoil using a fertilizer spreader. Rake the topsoil into the surface of the lawn and seed appropriately for the variety of turfgrass or turfgrass mix you have chosen. You may need to repeat this procedure over several years until your new grass overtakes and completely replaces the existing grass.

For large tracts, a sturdy lawn is one of the most attractive and economical groundcovers. To keep maintenance to a minimum, choose a hardy turfgrass that is slow growing, durable, and, if there are large trees on your property, adaptable to some shade.

green lawn running right up to the base of a towering tree is a beautiful sight and is common in many yards. Common, too, are the problems that many gardeners experience trying to maintain that area of lawn. Lawns and trees are not natural companions. Many trees cannot tolerate the amount of watering lawns require, and many lawns need more sun than a shady tree affords. Shallow-rooted trees often gobble up needed nutrients, leaving the lawn undernourished and prone to disease. All of these problems can be overcome with a bit of careful planning.

It starts with your critical choice of turfgrass. Avoid sun-loving varieties that simply will not grow properly in woodland and will result in a spindly, patchy—and very disappointing—result for the effort. Choose shade-tolerant turfgrasses, including fine-bladed fescues and perennial ryegrass of the cool-season varieties, and sturdy zoysia, St. Augustine grass, and Bahia grass of the warm-season varieties. If your woodland lawn is strongly lit in some spots and very shady in others, you can buy turf-seed mixes that combine sun- and shade-loving types.

As you might expect, shade lawns require some special care. You must keep the area raked clean of leaves so sunlight can reach the turf. Unlike a sun lawn, which is constantly thirsty due to evaporation, a shade lawn should be watered only when it looks dry. Fertilize half as much as you would a sunny lawn. When you mow, keep the blades at least 2 inches (50 mm) high, which will foster sturdier and greener growth, and never, ever mow a wet lawn. Finally, you might want to consider planting a flower bed around the base of each tree to give the yard a more finished look.

With the right type of lawn in place and the right maintenance regime, you soon will be reveling in the perfect woodland glade.

WOODLAND LAWNS

While turfgrass and trees are not natural companions, you can combine the two successfully by choosing shade-tolerant grass varieties. Consider planting some annual flower beds around the trees to provide a colorful transition between the two.

SOUTHERN LAWNS

If your summers are hot and your winters are warm, you're in the right location for warm-season grasses. They grow best in the entire southern Sunbelt, from Florida to Southern California, where the weather is either hot and humid or hot and dry and there's a decent supply of water. Warm-season grasses are vigorous growers and generally deep rooted because they search for moisture to offset the stress of the bright sun. While they thrive in summer, they often become dormant in winter—turn brown and cease growing—when they usually are overseeded with a temporary cover of cool-season grass, such as annual ryegrass or fescue.

There are several stand-out warm-season grasses. Bermuda grass, particularly hybrid Bermuda, is one of the most popular because of its affinity for heat, its durability, and its drought resistance. Bermuda does not tolerate shade, however. Bahia grass does, and likewise is a tough, traffic-resistant, coarse-bladed variety that is somewhat drought tolerant. St. Augustine grass tolerates both shade and sun better than any other warm-season grass and spreads quickly by surface rhizomes. It is coarse bladed and tends to develop thatch over time. Like Bermuda, St. Augustine grass needs to be overseeded in winter. Unlike most of the warm-season grasses, zoysia is fine and wiry but still can withstand traffic. It is very tolerant to drought, shade, and salt air, which makes it popular in coastal areas of Florida, the Gulf, and Southern California. Of the warm-season grasses, it also is one of the least susceptible to pests and diseases.

You can plant any of these warm-season wonders by themselves, but for maximum hardiness, consider a southern-lawn mixture, which is a combination of one or more grass varieties.

Warm-season grasses, with their deep roots and vigorous growth habits, are perfectly suited to southern weather conditions, which can include both heat and drought. Since they tend to go dormant in winter, overseeding with a cool-season grass will maintain a green expanse year-round.

ACTIVITY LAWNS

Lawns and childhood just seem to go hand in hand in our memories. As any child—or former child—can tell you, lawns are best used for play. A well-tended, carefully chosen turfgrass lawn is the perfect activity surface. It's soft and cushiony to absorb rough-and-tumble play, it holds up under the abuse of many pairs of sneakered feet, and it smells so good when you fall down on it.

Not all turfgrasses, however, are up to the challenge. Play flag football on Colonial bent grass, for example, and you'll have a ruined lawn in no time. Play fetch for half an hour with a big dog on a springtime field of first-growth annual ryegrass and your lawn will look as if it were mangled by a hailstorm. When activity is the purpose, or at least the predominant purpose of your lawn, install a turfgrass that's up to the challenge.

There are a handful of turfgrasses that can stand up to high traffic. Of the warm-season grasses, Bermuda grass is perhaps the best all-around athletic surface, which is why it turns up on baseball diamonds, football fields, and golf course fairways. It is drought resistant and deep rooted. Bermuda's only drawback is that it doesn't tolerate shade well, but that usually isn't an issue for an activity lawn. Another fine warm-season turfgrass is St. Augustine grass, which easily stands up to that big dog and tolerates heat and shade. Fine-textured zoysia is yet another strong warm-season grass. Among the cool-season grasses, tall fescue rates high on the durability scale, as does perennial ryegrass.

High-activity lawns take special care. If you're in the market for an especially high-activity lawn, ask for some of the new "sports turf" blends adapted to your area that are formulated to take a pounding.

If you have children or pets or both, your lawn takes an extra pounding. Special turfgrass blends, such as sports turf, are designed for high wear and tear; fescues for cool season and Bermuda grass for warm season are other sturdy options.

NON-TURF LAWNS

To many, a lawn is little more than an expanse of turfgrass, and a little boring at that. Increasingly, gardeners are looking for alternatives to turfgrass, sometimes to cut down on yard maintenance, sometimes to preserve scarce water resources, and sometimes just to add a whole new look to a front- or backyard. Non-turf lawns, fashioned from low-growing groundcovers, are not grasses at all but low-growing plants with spreading growth habits. Planted in plugs or individually at regular intervals, groundcover plants soon grow together to form a uniform surface. Plants classified as groundcovers can grow from as little as a few inches (approximately 13 cm) to as much as 2 feet (60 cm) tall. Some of the low-growing species even can take some foot traffic and truly will function as a turfgrass substitute.

(Above and top) Low-growing groundcovers are an increasingly popular alternative to the traditional turfgrass lawn, especially when time and resources are limited. They add an interesting design element to any architectural style, from Victorian to Mediterranean.

One of the pluses of groundcovers is that a large number of varieties can grow happily where many turfgrasses struggle, such as in medium to deep shade and on slopes, where it is difficult or even hazardous to mow. In addition, groundcovers generally need less maintenance—their dense growth tends to stifle weeds, and once established they require less fertilizing.

The major benefit of many (though not all) groundcovers is that they tend to need less watering since the spread of the leaves retains soil moisture. This dynamic has made native groundcovers a particularly popular choice for xeriscaping, the practice of using environmentally compatible native plants that have minimal watering requirements.

Groundcovers are uniquely adaptable plants: the charming steps to this home are formed entirely from dense mats of low-growing groundcover.

Many varieties of turfgrass can take a pounding, but none can withstand the repeated pressure of automobile traffic. The weight crushes the blades and compacts the ground—mercilessly. For years, the only option was to pave driveways. Then, a new generation of synthetic pavers and subsurface plastic honeycomb supports made a car-proof lawn possible.

TURF PAVEMENT

Pavers, gridlike precast blocks with holes that can be formed into diamond- or square-shaped patterns, are set edge to edge, flush to the soil surface, then filled with soil and either seeded or planted with grass or low-growing groundcover. The taller the turf is allowed to grow, the more the pavers are hidden—the look is up to you. Plastic honeycombs can be employed in much the same way as pavers but are designed to provide totally invisible support under a covering of turfgrass or groundcover. Both options give you a green pathway to your home's parking area.

Precast pavers and plastic honeycomb grids can be used for any high-traffic areas in your yard that need support, not just car areas. Consider it for the children's biking route (though a regular lawn will provide better cushion if they should take a tumble), the dog run, or a pathway from one area of the garden to another or from a sidewalk to a garden dining area. For softening the effects of hardscape, there is no better alternative than turf pavement.

(Above) Rough-cut stone blocks create an appealing driveway, but turf pavement can be used to soften any garden hardscape.

(Left) While they take some care and expertise to install, synthetic pavers and subsurface support systems pay off handsomely in beauty and durability.

W hen planning any work on your lawn—whether restoring, replanting grass, or planting groundcover—first take some time to think about a few key issues. The mental work you do now can save you hours of unnecessary physical labor and make the endeavor more successful and pleasurable.

In this chapter, we'll provide you with questions to ask and issues to consider that will help you address your specific lawn situation. First, think about your needs, both geographically and within your yard. Next, consider the purpose you want your lawn to serve. If you already have turfgrass, you'll learn how to decide whether to restore it or install a new lawn. The size you want the area to be also is an important consideration, since the scale will help determine the type of turfgrass or groundcover you install and the amount of time, resources, and energy it will take to keep it up.

Whether you intend to restore or replant, you need to know a good deal about the condition of your soil, including its fertility, acid-to-alkaline balance, and composition. Watering is another consideration. Does your present irrigation system provide adequate coverage, or will you need to make adjustments prior to restoring or installing a new lawn?

Part of your decision-making also includes the tools and materials you'll need for lawn installation, routine maintenance, or both, including fertilizers and herbicides.

As you go through the questions, keep a pad of paper handy. Some answers will be easy; others will require a bit more thought or even some investigative work. When you can answer them all, you'll have a plan that's ready to be put into action.

Lawns are long-term commitments, requiring some careful thought before making a final choice

A Planting Checklist

A perfect lawn takes some work, but, more important, it takes some planning, which includes an understanding of your climate and soil conditions as well as your needs and resources.

CHOOSING LAWNS AND GROUNDCOVERS

The universe of turfgrasses is divided simply into cool-season turfgrasses that grow mainly in northern climates, where winters are cold and summers are temperate or warm and moist; and warm-season turfgrasses, which are largely southern, thriving in mild-winter and hot-summer climates.

For example, do you live in the Pacific Coast region, from Vancouver down to just north of Los Angeles? If so, cool-season grasses are for you, sown or sodded in early spring to late autumn. Do you live in the northern Gulf states or Southern California? You have a choice of cool- and warm-season grasses, depending on your local climate, but you may want to use drought-resistant turf in drier areas and think about overseeding warm-season turf in the winter. Are you in the desert southwest? Use only warm-season turfgrasses, and since you will be working with alkaline soil, you may need to acidify its pH lightly to promote thriving growth. Do you live in the Rocky Mountains, Midwest, or central Canada? Most folks in these regions use cool-season grasses that are seeded August to September or lay sod March through October. Extreme southern parts of this region may be able to tolerate a warm-season grass with a winter overseeding of cool-season grass. If you live in the eastern

midsection of the United States, from parts of Oklahoma to Virginia and the northern parts of North Carolina, you have the option of either warm- or cool-season grasses and need to water only to supplement rainfall. Do you live in the Northeast? Cool-season grasses are the best, and the acidic soil likely needs little or no amendments for pH balance. Sow your grass in late summer or early spring and plant sod April to the first frost. If you live somewhere in the Southeast, from the Gulf Coast to Florida, or in Hawaii, only warm-season grasses will be suitable, and you must be vigilant with lawn care in these hot, humid climates to prevent fungal disease.

The type of turfgrass or turfgrass blend you purchase will depend to a great extent on where you live. Cool-season grasses grow best in moist, mostly northern climates where winters are cold. Warm-season grasses flourish in hot and dry southern climates.

Perhaps the most basic question to ask yourself when choosing a turfgrass or groundcover is: what will be its purpose? Are you looking for an activity surface that will withstand your play and that of children and pets? Do you want it to be purely ornamental—a visual delight, with little anticipated foot traffic? Do you want to create a pathway that leads from one area to another in the yard? Do you want a lawn that will endure automobile traffic? The answers to these questions will help determine your grass and groundcover options.

The more ornamental your choice, the finer the quality of grass or groundcover you will want to select. If your child's flag football team has regular practice at the house, you still can host a lawn with rugged beauty by planting one of the "sports turf" mixes. You also can choose several lawn and groundcover varieties for distinct areas of your property, all serving different purposes. Your choices should be governed by your expectations for use.

An attractive lawn can serve as a refreshing outdoor "dining room" during the summertime.

As you assess your needs, ask one more question: how much time do you want to spend, not only to plant but also to maintain your choices? Ornamental lawns can require significantly more nurturing than utility lawns. Groundcovers initially can be more expensive than turfgrass and most cannot survive much foot traffic, but they generally require less maintenance.

Keep these considerations in mind before choosing.

The amount of wear and tear you expect your lawn to tolerate should determine the type of turfgrass you choose. Hardy strains work best for high-activity lawns.

SCALING THE PROJECT

Whether you are restoring an existing lawn or installing a new one, step back for a minute and really look at the area. Is it huge—or not big enough? You want a good sense of proportion—of lawn to house and of lawn to surrounding landscape. A small house swimming in a ballpark-size lawn may work in areas where properties generally are big, but that look doesn't work in typical city or suburban tracts. Is your backyard a massive lawn framed by a scrawny border of flowers and trees? Conversely, is your lawn so truncated that it is nearly swallowed up by huge swells of the same? The perfect time to rectify these proportional errors is now.

If you perceive that you have too much lawn, try working in some flower beds, a spot for a small stand of trees, or some well-placed garden sculptures. You also can diminish the size of the lawn effectively without losing the sense of a green expanse by carving out swaths and planting groundcover for a change of texture. If you have too little lawn and too much flower bed, scale back the beds and extend your lawn or create a transition with groundcover. Sketch out your yard at a scale of approximately ¼ inch (6 mm) for every foot (30 cm). Start playing with the elements—trees, flower borders, and lawn area. Even the roughest drawings can give you ideas as you doodle.

Thinking about scale also means giving thought to the scope of the project. The bigger the lawn, the more time consuming and labor intensive it will be.

Scaling the size of your lawn to your house (left) is an important consideration when planting or restoring. Try breaking up large lawn areas with sweeping flower beds (top) or walkways.

If you have an existing lawn, ask yourself this: is my lawn salvageable, or do I need to start all over again? You might want to restore rather than replace your lawn if somewhere between 20 and 40 percent of it is dead; has spindly, sparse growth; or the same percentages of it are covered with broadleaf or grassy weeds [see Eliminating Broadleaf Weeds, pg. 56]. Renovation also may be possible if your lawn is overly spongy and is filled with thatch. Dethatching is a relatively simple process of removing the dead grass from your lawn [see Dethatching, pg. 66]. On the other hand, if more than 50 percent of your lawn is dead, bare ground, or filled with weeds, and your soil is so hard and compacted a screwdriver can bounce off it, you probably should scrap the whole lawn and start from scratch.

Before restoration, figure out why the lawn deteriorated in the first place. Was it not dethatched, aerated, fertilized, or watered properly? Renovation is the time to correct all of the correctable problems. At this point, determine whether you want to take on the whole job, only part of it, or have a lawn-care specialist help or take care of it for you. If you choose the latter, be sure to get several detailed bids for the job [see Professional Lawn Services, pg. 82].

If you decide to install a new lawn, you have even more decisions to make—but you also have more opportunities. You can choose a turfgrass for precisely your purpose and budget, and you can decide to change the rest of your landscape in the process, creating new flower beds or otherwise changing your yard's configuration.

Once you've made these decisions, turn to the type of turfgrass you want to install and the method of installation—be it reseeding, laying in sod, or planting plugs. These latter considerations are important because the type of grass you want

INSTALLING OR RESTORING

may not be available in all planting choices. There are pros and cons for each type of installation—for example, reseeding is much cheaper than laying in sod, but sod squelches weeds and gives you an instant lawn; the cost of planting plugs or sprigs lies in between but requires more labor. Consider all of these issues before moving forward.

Whether to restore or replant is the key decision. If the problem spots are small and localized, you may be able to reseed those areas. If trouble spots are widespread, however, replanting may be in order.

ASSESSING SOIL CONDITIONS

Soil is the cradle of your lawn, determining to a large extent the health of the turfgrass it nurtures. Understanding the composition and condition of your soil so that you can assess improvements properly and add the right amendments is crucial to creating a productive growth medium and successful lawn.

Assessing your soil involves two questions: what is the state of your soil and what type of soil does the turfgrass or groundcover you're considering prefer? For existing soil, you first want to know its density—whether it is light, sandy soil or sandy loam, which is quick draining but holds few nutrients; or if it is dense clay or clay loam, which holds moisture but is so hard that tender grass roots have a tough time penetrating to take hold. Both are undesirable and require correction.

The best way to determine your soil type, whether for restoration or new installation purposes, is to perform a percolation test [see Percolation Testing, pg. 28]. You can get a clue to your soil's content simply by picking up a handful of it and making a fist. When you open your hand, does the soil sift through your fingers, stick together, or crumble lightly? No matter what type of soil you turn out to have, it's equally as important to find out if it is compacted—that is, compressed by foot traffic or other use so that it lacks essential oxygen for plant growth, has few microbes or earthworms to help keep it fertile and aerated, and is too dense for any roots to penetrate. If this is the case, you will need to aerate your soil before planting [see Aerating, pg. 68].

Most turfgrasses thrive in a slightly acid soil that has a pH between 6.5 and 7.0. Various methods exist for determining your soil's acid-alkaline pH balance, including home soil test kits and portable pH meters.

Another consideration is your soil's pH level, or its acid-alkaline balance, which is measured on a scale of 1 to 14. The lower the number is below midpoint 7.0, the more acidic the soil. Lawns generally require a slightly acidic soil, with a pH level of 6.5–7.0. If your pH level is below 6.5, it is simply too acidic for most lawns and you'll need to add ground limestone to "sweeten" the soil. If your soil tests over 7.0, you'll need to increase the acid level, or "sour" the soil, by working in sulfur. To determine your soil's pH level, conduct a soil test [see Assessing Your Soil and Site, pg. 26].

Last, study a clump of your soil for fertility—its humus content, or amount of decayed organic matter, and its nutrients. Insufficient humus is indicated by soil that is a pale brown or red and does not hold together well. The presence, or absence, of the three essential nutrients—nitrogen, phosphorus, and potassium—can be determined to some extent simply by looking at your existing lawn. A soil test also will reveal the specific nutrient imbalances and recommend corrective actions.

Yellowed grass indicates poor nitrogen content; thin, weak growth and a reddish-purple tinge to grass blades can mean too little phosphorus; and grass with brown tips and yellow veining can be a result of too little potassium. These nutrients can be added, but it's crucial that the area be properly aerated to receive them. In addition, you may want to encourage earthworms and microbes in the soil by adding compost, which contains abundant organic matter.

Once you understand the soil you have, research the soil requirements of the turfgrass or groundcover you want.

The fact of the matter is, lawns are water guzzlers. The move to native grasses and certain groundcovers largely comes from a growing consciousness of water as a precious, and increasingly rare, resource. Drought can occur anywhere, so it's important to develop a strategy for how to keep your lawn watered properly.

WATERING

First, evaluate how much water your new or renovated lawn needs. If you don't have an in-ground, automated watering system you may want to consider installing one. If you already have an in-ground system, evaluate if it is doing the job adequately. If your lawn is lush in parts and nearly brown in others, your sprinkler pattern may be at fault, or you may not have enough sprinkler heads. Set out a series of open-mouth jars or pie pans at different points in your lawn and turn on the system for fifteen minutes. Check the depth of water in each container. The levels will tell you where adequate water is falling and where it is not.

Also, is the water penetrating deep enough? Water for half an hour, then dig down to see how far it has penetrated. A healthy lawn should be moist down to about 5 inches (13 cm). This depth of watering encourages the grass to send its roots deep into the soil, where they will be less prone to moisture loss and disease. It takes about ¼ inch (6 mm) of water in sandy soil, and 1¾ inches (4.5 cm) in clay, to penetrate to that depth. If your lawn is not receiving the proper penetration of water, consider watering longer—half an hour to 45 minutes—fewer times a week, which will keep soil-moisture content high down deep where it counts.

Think about your watering practices. Watering should be done between 4 a.m. and 8 a.m. to allow the lawn to absorb sufficient moisture before the sun's rays cause evaporation. Watering in the evening can cause a lawn to stay too wet and possibly develop fungal disease.

The amount of water your lawn will require depends not only on your climate and the season but the type of turfgrass you select. Some, such as certain fescues and Bermuda grass, are very drought tolerant.

CHOOSING TURFGRASS OR GROUNDCOVER

Perhaps the most fundamental question to ask yourself as you contemplate restoring your lawn is whether to have a lawn at all. In general, groundcovers are cheaper and far easier to maintain, requiring less watering, fertilizing, and absolutely no mowing, and there's far less chance of disease, pests, or drought decimating them. You still may want a lawn, but if time and resources are short, you might consider cutting back on the size to incorporate a bed of groundcover.

If you decide that at least some lawn is the way to go, the easy part is done. The tougher decision is what type of lawn to plant, keeping in mind your geographical location, which determines whether you should choose a warm-season or cool-season grass. The other issues to consider are those discussed in this chapter and summarized in the Lawns and Groundcovers Planning Flowchart [see pg. 22].

Turfgrasses come in single varieties or cultivars of one type, blends of different varieties of the same species, and mixes of different types of grasses. Some specialty mixtures address specific conditions or purposes—for example, a shady lawn, a "luxury" lawn for show, or "sports turf" for high-activity areas. Explore the range of possibilities before you choose and factor in how important the method of installation is to you. Some grass varieties are only available in seed or in sod, and others, particularly the blends and mixes, seldom are available in sod.

If you decide you want to install some groundcover or replace your lawn entirely with groundcover, the questions to ask are similar. Do you want to be able to walk on your groundcover, or will you treat it like a flower bed? Is the area in sun or shade? Is water ever a scarce resource? Is your region prone to summer fires, where a natural fire break is not only pretty but practical? Do you want an all-green groundcover or one that is colorful and flowering? Are you intending to plant your groundcover on a slope, in a rock garden, in between paving stones of a pathway, or other special locations? The answers to all these questions will help narrow your choices.

In addition, you may want to consult with a local lawn specialist, your agricultural extension office, and even such generalist organizations as the Lawn Institute. Armed with the information these sources have to offer, you'll be ready to head out to your local nursery, garden center, or sod farm and make your purchases.

Sod is grown and purchased from sod farms, usually located in rural areas, where long strips are cut only to order by special harvesting machines on the day of delivery.

Once you've decided whether to restore or replace your existing lawn, or if you are installing a lawn for the first time, you'll need a source for your turfgrass. Your choice—from seed, sod, plugs, or sprigs—will send you to different sources.

Seed is the least expensive method of planting turfgrass, which means the larger your area, the more likely you will want to use seed. Various mail order and online catalogs offer seed in just about every variety you can imagine. You may be better off consulting your local nursery, garden retail center, or lawn-care center, which will stock only those varieties proven to thrive in your region. They also will have all-purpose mixes of turfgrass species. It is worth calling around to different suppliers if you have in mind a special mix such as a part sun, part shade turfgrass or a wear-resistant sports turf. Your local agricultural extension office also may be able to offer assistance and advice.

To purchase sod, plugs, or sprigs, visit a turf farm. Turf farms are what the name implies—large farms devoted to growing a single crop: turfgrass. They usually are located in rural areas and cut their turf only to order. If you aren't sure about the type of turfgrass you'd like and want to see a few varieties, it's worth the trip to take a look at these remarkable establishments. Before you head out, however, make sure that they accommodate consumer visits.

Most warm-season turf farms carry not just sod but sprigs and plugs as well. When you see a turfgrass that suits your fancy, ask a series of questions: Will this grass grow in my area? Is it wear resistant and how do I maintain it? Will it go dormant in winter and require overseeding? Is it susceptible to any particular pests or diseases? How often should it be mowed, and how high?

Before you make any purchase, ask about the product guarantee. Be sure that you have replacement rights if it should fail after installation.

SOURCES FOR TURFGRASS

Before choosing turfgrass, decide whether you want to sow seed or lay sod, since not all turfgrasses are available in both forms.

TOOLS AND MATERIALS

Routine lawn care demands its share of special tools; lawn restoration and installation require still others. Beyond that, which tools you use likely will depend on the size of your lawn area.

To restore an existing lawn, you'll need a thatching, or dethatching, rake, which features knifelike blades designed to cut through dead grass growth; for a large lawn, consider renting a power dethatcher. Aerate your lawn by punching deep holes at regular intervals in the surface to allow for better water and nutrient penetration and to add oxygen to the lawn at root level; again, if your lawn is expansive, you may want to rent a gas-powered aerator, which deposits the short plugs on your lawn's surface as compost. You'll also need a spreader, a multipurpose tool that evenly broadcasts fertilizers, amendments, and seed.

If you are installing a new lawn, you may want to rent a gas-powered sod cutter to break away existing sod at the roots. You'll likely need to rent a power rototiller as well, to break up compacted soil, and a lawn roller to level and firm the soil before planting. You also may want to rent a power seeder, which cuts grooves into the soil and evenly deposits lawn seed in them.

For general lawn maintenance, you first and foremost need a good mower. A gasoline-powered rotary mower is the number one choice of most homeowners; a mulching model chops up the grass and delivers clippings as mulch. Reel mowers are still a popular choice due to cost and the action of the blades, which delivers an exceptionally sharp cut. A good edge trimmer also is essential to lawn maintenance; choose between gasoline-powered or manual models. String trimmers are best saved for lawn edges that abut hardscaping.

Other handy tools include a garden cart, lawn and leaf rakes, spades and shovels, shears, a weeder, sprayers for herbicides and fungicides, and a good, non-twisting hose that reaches the expanse of your lawn.

Finally, you will want to investigate the range of irrigation systems to find the one that best serves the needs of your landscape.

Equipment needed to tend and maintain a lawn range from the power aerator, dethatcher, and lawn mower to the simple multi-toothed rake, handy for removing leaves from the lawn's surface so the grass blades can grow thick and strong.

A Garden cart
B Grass shears
C Lawn rake
D Lawn edger
E String trimmer
F Dethatching rake
G Hand edger

TOOLS AND MATERIALS
FOR LAWNS AND GROUNDCOVERS

For Renovating an Existing Lawn

Dethatcher, manual or power:
Knifelike blades cut out dead grass

Aerator, manual or power:
Punches deep holes at regular intervals to allow for better penetration of water and nutrients and to add oxygen at root level; extracted plugs can be used as compost for the lawn surface

Spreader, drop or rotary:
Deposits fertilizers, amendments, or seed in paths the width of the spreader (drop) or in a circular pattern (rotary)

For Installing a New Lawn

Power sod cutter:
Breaks away existing sod at the roots

Power rotary tiller:
Breaks up compacted soil before planting

Roller, lawn or water:
Water-filled roller levels and firms the soil before planting

Power seeder:
Cuts grooves into the soil and evenly deposits seed in them

For General Lawn Maintenance

Mower, reel or gas-powered rotary
Trimmers, edge, turf, and string
Garden cart
Rakes, lawn and leaf
Spades
Shovels
Shears
Weeder
Sprayer, hand-held or backpack
Non-twisting hose
Sprinkler system, automatic or hose-end

LAWNS AND GROUNDCOVERS PLANNING FLOWCHART

A flowchart is a written checklist that allows you to quickly scan the major decisions that should be reviewed as you consider a garden project. The one illustrated here specifically deals with the decisions gardeners must make when they undertake planting or restoring lawns or groundcovers. A few minutes spent with the checklist will ensure you remember each waypoint to a successful project. Refer to the checklist before beginning—it will save you time, effort, and money.

1 **Site Choice Questions:**
Where is your yard located, both geographically and within your environs? What is its exposure to light and to shade? Are you restoring an existing lawn, or deciding whether to plant new turfgrass, groundcover, or both? How does your scheme fit in with existing pathways, trees, and other plantings? Depending on your region, can you overseed during winter or will your lawn go dormant? What is the hardiness of the turfgrass or groundcover you're considering?

DETERMINING YOUR OBJECTIVES

2 **Goal Questions:**
What purpose do you want your lawn to serve? Do you want an activity surface that will withstand children, pets, and outdoor parties? Do you want an "ornamental" lawn, with little anticipated foot traffic? Do you want a turf pavement that will stand up to automobile traffic? How much time will planning and designing require? When do you want the project finished? How much ongoing care will your new lawn need?

PLANNING FOR THE PROJECT

ALLOCATING TIME AND SCHEDULING

3 **Scale Questions:**
Is your space wide and wandering? Do you want to accentuate the dimensions of your space, or diminish it? Are you seeking to complement or contrast with the style of your house through your choice of turfgrass or groundcover? Are you thinking about changing any other features of your yard at the same time? Will your project require special equipment, how much time will it take, and will you need assistance to complete it?

4 **Plant Selection Questions:** What are the growth habits, care needs, and color display features of the turfgrasses or groundcovers you're considering? Does your planned space support those requirements? What kind of sun and shade exposure does it receive? What type of soil does it have? If laying sod or planting plugs, do they look healthy and free of pests in the garden store or at the sod farm? If sowing seed, how large is the selection, and does it include seed mixes? Are the garden store and sod farm staff knowledgeable and helpful? When new sod arrives, does it appear fresh and well watered? Will the supplier stand behind the quality of the sod should it fail? What are the retailers' replacement policies?

PREPARING TO PURCHASE TURFGRASSES OR GROUNDCOVERS

SOIL PREPARATION, MATERIALS, AND TOOLS

5 **Preparation Questions:** What is the quality of your soil? Is it loose, or hard, compacted clay? Does it drain quickly and stay dry most of the time, or does it drain slowly and stay boggy? Do you know your soil 's pH level or do you need to test it? What materials, supplies, tools, and amendments will you require? What fertilizers will you need for the lawn or groundcover you're considering? Will it require any special type of irrigation system? To which kinds of pests and diseases is your desired lawn prone, and what type of preventive measures can you employ?

FINDING HELP AND INFORMATION

6 **Resource and Aid Questions:** Where will you turn for expert advice? Do you have current catalogs, periodicals, and books containing information about the lawns and planting techniques you will require? Does your garden retailer have knowledgeable staff able to assist you in your decisions and answer questions? Do you know the hardiness of the lawn or groundcover you're considering? Are you familiar with online electronic resources, or do you have access to your agricultural extension office agent? Are gardening classes available through educators in your area? Are there local experts who broadcast on radio or television to whom you may turn for questions and advice?

You've decided to take the big leap—plant an entirely new lawn. Preparing for the installation is every bit as important as the installation itself, and it begins with evaluating your soil's texture, drainage, and fertility.

In this chapter, we'll tell you how to examine your soil, collect a soil sample for testing, and read the results. A percolation test—checking how long it takes water to be absorbed in a hole dug in the ground—is a quick and reliable way to determine if you have a soil drainage problem.

Planting a new lawn is the perfect time to install an in-ground sprinkler system and lighting system if you don't already have them. We'll take you through those processes as well as some design options. At the same time, you may want to consider putting in a mow strip between your lawn edge and flower beds to make mowing easier and complete the border. We'll show you how to accomplish it.

Finally, you probably will need to amend your soil before installing your new lawn. We'll tell you how to choose your amendments and how to till them into the soil; we'll also discuss the new generation of landscape fabrics that act as weed barriers for newly planted groundcover beds.

With this prep work under your belt, you'll be ready to install your new lawn—with nearly assured success.

> Good planning matches your soil's texture and fertility to your choice of turfgrass or groundcover

Preparing to Plant

A lawn planted in groundcover makes a lush, romantic statement. Groundcovers are generally easier to maintain, require less watering, and of course no mowing. In addition, many are shade tolerant.

ASSESSING YOUR SOIL AND SITE

A lawn reflects the quality of the soil underneath. If the soil is deficient in major nutrients, compacted so that water cannot penetrate properly, or so sandy that it can't hold onto water for long, you will see these conditions expressed in sparse and patchy growth or yellowed and weak blades of grass. A deep-green, thick, and thriving lawn, on the other hand, is a testament to a healthy soil base below, one likely filled with nutrients, of the right texture, and containing a flourishing microbe and earthworm population generating rich organic matter. Good lawn soil is fertile with humus, holds water yet drains well, and is neither too sandy nor too claylike.

Few gardeners are blessed with loam, the best of all possible soils, but you can bring yours close to that ideal texture, pH level, and nutrient content with some amending. To decide which amendments you need, start with a simple soil test.

There are a couple of ways to have your soil tested. One is to use a home test kit [see opposite], the other is to send off a soil sample to a lab recommended by your local agricultural extension office or garden retailer.

Test kits differ in some respects, but all of them break down the three key nutrients—nitrogen, potassium, and phosphorus—and the minor, or trace nutrients, such as manganese, copper, zinc, and iron, that are present in your soil. For the major nutrients, a good test kit not only will tell you the reading but also indicate the measured level of each compared with an ideal standard. For example, if the test results indicate that your soil's nitrogen level is 0.2, with 1.0 being the optimum amount of nitrogen the soil should contain, you'll know that your soil has only 20 percent of the nitrogen content to support your lawn and that you'll need to supplement with a high-nitrogen amendment.

The results also will tell you the pH level of your soil—that is, the acid to alkaline balance, which is as critical a component as nutrient level. Most turfgrasses prefer a slightly acidic level between 6.5 and 7.0 pH to flourish; below 6.5, the soil is too acid; above 7.0, the soil is too alkaline for good grass growth. Your pH result may indicate that you need to add sulfur to acidify the soil or lime to de-acidify it. The pH analysis also may indicate the amount of lime in the soil. Too much lime can restrict your attempts to acidify a soil's pH balance because it absorbs sulfur, so you will need to add more than normal to achieve your desired result. The analysis also might indicate that your soil has too much sodium, or salt build-up, which can be caused naturally by soil minerals, your local water supply, or excess use of salt-based fertilizers. Too much salinity can cause leaf burn and kill your lawn before it has a chance to grow. To cure this condition, you may need to add gypsum followed by a thorough watering to leach out the salts.

Whichever test method you use, you will be ready to amend.

Soil test kits measure the levels of the three major nutrients— nitrogen, potassium, and phosphorus—in your soil, as well as its pH, or acid-alkaline balance. Most test kits also provide advice on which amendments to use to improve your soil's condition.

COLLECTING A SOIL-TEST SAMPLE

Soil tests measure the nutrients and acid-alkaline balance (pH) of your soil. Soil testers are available as electronic meters or test kits sold by garden retailers or mail order by soil laboratories. Both methods produce equally reliable test results, provided you take care to acquire a good sample. Follow the procedure shown for best results:

2 Using a clean trowel and disposable cup, take the sample from the side of the hole to avoid collecting surface soil that may have fallen into the hole.

3 Repeat the collection process with a new, clean cup for each of the test holes, if more than one.

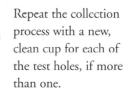

1 Dig a hole at least 16 in. (40 cm) wide and deep in the area to be tested. If the area is large, dig test holes in several different locations.

4 On a clean sheet of paper, combine and thoroughly mix the samples from each cup to make one uniform mixed sample.

5 Place the sample in a clean, sealable plastic bag for transport to either a laboratory or the site where you will perform the analysis from a home test kit.

PERCOLATION TESTING

Few things are more important to the successful cultivation of any lawn than proper soil texture and drainage. Turfgrasses simply won't grow well in boggy, soggy conditions—the roots will rot, the grass will yellow, and you will be disappointed with the results. Turfgrasses also won't thrive when planted over dense hardpan or clay—yielding thin, scraggly, and patchy growth at best.

The great advantage of planting a new lawn is that you can test the soil easily to check drainage conditions. You should perform this test in several different spots, however, since you likely will get differing results. For example, areas that receive high traffic will have more compacted soil than the rest of the yard, and areas near trees may be clogged from surface roots.

The basic drainage test is called a percolation test, and it works the way it sounds. You test to see how long it takes a quantity of water to percolate, or seep, into the ground, then drain away. This test couldn't be easier.

About noon on a day that is moderately temperate, pick out several spots in the area you've planned for your lawn and dig holes 2 feet (60 cm) deep and 1–2 feet (30–60 cm) wide. Fill them with water and make a note of the time. The water level should drop at a rate of about 1–2 inches (25–50 mm) per hour. Faster or slower drainage of irrigation water is not ideal for turfgrass.

Around dinnertime, make a check of the holes. If they are completely drained, you have sandy soil, and you will need to amend before planting to improve water retention. If the holes have not drained completely, right before bedtime take a flashlight with you and again check the holes. If they have not drained completely by then, you have claylike soil, and you will need to amend to improve drainage.

Whether your soil is claylike or sandy, supplementing with compost or organic amendments is a must since both conditions deprive a lawn of nutrients. With sandy soil that drains too quickly, important nutrients are quickly washed away from the plant's roots and the lawn becomes subject to drought. With claylike soil, nutrients are prevented from adequately reaching roots and growth is stunted. If your soil is compacted, which is more common in lawn areas where organic matter has slowly decomposed, you may want to mix some fine peat moss with one or two parts playground sand and apply the mix to the lawn area.

Water should penetrate your soil readily, as is the case shown here. For any lawn, claylike soil needs to be lightened to improve drainage; sandy soil needs to be amended to improve water retention. Both benefit from added organic matter.

CONDUCTING A PERCOLATION TEST

Percolation is a fancy word for absorption. It measures the rate at which water is absorbed by soil, or flows through it. Lawns are especially prone to having dense soil because they are left in place for many years and their natural organic components decay and wash away, leaving only mineral components behind. Soil that is too dense will fail to absorb water and may be prone to runoff during heavy rains. Soil that is too loose will have the opposite problem—water will flow right through, leaving the lawn with too little water and fewer nutrients. Withhold water from your lawn for several days, then check its percolation rate by performing this simple test:

2 If the lawn area is large, dig holes in several spots that receive different foot traffic and light exposure, and test each.

1 Dig a hole 1–2 ft. (30–60 cm) wide and 2 ft. (60 cm) deep in an area of your lawn.

3 Fill the holes with water to their rims, noting on a piece of paper the time each was filled.

4 After several hours, note the level of the water in each hole. Soil with proper texture will drain at the rate of 1–2 in. (25–50 mm) per hour.

INSTALLING AN IN-GROUND IRRIGATION SYSTEM

Permanent watering systems make caring for a lawn easier. Installing such systems, while physically demanding, is easy to do and requires basic tools. Plan your system carefully, using the readily available literature and worksheets at your garden retail or hardware store. Allow for future expansion. Follow these simple steps to automate irrigation of your lawn:

2 Cut pipe to length, using a PVC pipe-cutting tool, then join sections using two-step primer and adhesive. Allow the joints to dry.

3 Where each irrigation head is planned, install a 90° "street tee" or "ell" fitting with slip joints to the pipe and a threaded coupler to the riser.

1 Install a separate control valve for each water circuit. Use a ½-in. (12-mm) reducing bushing between each valve and the lines that run to the sprinkler heads or drip emitters.

4 Install sprinkler spray housings or drip-system hose couplers atop each riser, using three wraps of Teflon tape around each threaded fitting. Turn on the water and adjust each sprinkler.

5 Set sprinklers to water early in the morning so the grass has time to dry before nightfall.

INSTALLING OUTDOOR LIGHTING

The addition of outdoor 12-volt lighting to your lawn landscape is a finishing touch that pays big dividends in safety and beauty. Many different models and styles of outdoor fixtures are available from hardware stores and home centers, as well as garden retailers; pick one that complements your home's architecture. Installing a low-voltage system is simple and hazard free. Follow the steps shown for a successful project that will beautify your yard:

2 Attach the fixture to the main wire with a fastening clip that pierces its conductors. After attaching the fixture, bury the wire and close the trench.

1 Install low-voltage wiring when you install sprinklers, or trench and lay wire from the controller transformer at a convenient, grounded, GFI-protected outdoor receptacle to the lighting fixture.

4 Most transformers have timers that automatically turn the lighting system on and off. Set the clock to the desired on and off times.

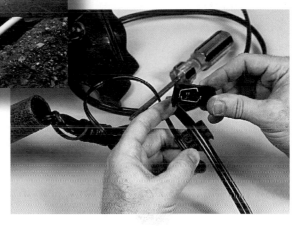

3 After the fixture is attached and the circuit is completed, attach the main wire to the 12-volt transformer with waterproof wire nuts.

MOW STRIPS AND BORDERS

As anyone who's mowed a lawn can tell you, the edges are the toughest part to keep trim. Flower-bed plantings often spill out onto lawns, making it difficult to get a fine edge without inflicting damage on adjacent plants. You also might have one of the more-aggressive grasses, such as St. Augustine grass or Bermuda grass, which over time can invade your beds.

What you need is a demilitarized zone of sorts between your lawn and your beds, where a mower can traverse safely to cut the lawn's edge without cutting up half of your annuals and perennials. Mow strips, or upright borders created with vinyl or wood benderboard, vinyl, aluminum, or ironwork, can make mowing lawn edges infinitely easier. They also provide a finishing touch that can add greatly to your garden's appearance and even enhance a style such as an English country border or a Mediterranean garden.

Mow strips, which generally run at least 6 inches (15 cm) wide, can be fashioned from a number of different materials—concrete, brick, masonry blocks or pavers, or wood. They all are installed in roughly the same way [see opposite].

Installing benderboard is less labor intensive but still creates a visual break between beds and lawn. These borders are less protective of your plants, since no real "mowing zone" is created, but the benefit is that they are not as permanent—if you want to change the shape of lawn or planting bed, all you need to do is pick up the benderboard and re-place it. The drawback of benderboard is that the materials tend to deteriorate over time with exposure to the elements.

You also can purchase different types of decorative borders, typically in 6-to-12-inch (15-to-30-cm) lengths, made from cast aluminum, cast iron, terra cotta, or stone. For these, you will need to dig a narrow trench deep enough so that when the pieces are inserted the tops are level with the ground.

Whether you choose to install a mow strip or a border, these additions will make your mowing chores easier while becoming attractive features in your yard.

Mow strips make cutting lawn along flower beds and borders infinitely easier, while protecting plantings from becoming accidental victims of mower blades. They also lend a finished appearance to the landscape.

INSTALLING MOW STRIPS

Install mow strips to make lawn maintenance easier and create separation between the turfgrass and adjacent flower beds and shrub landscaping. Any durable material will give a good result—concrete, brick, stone, vinyl, or wooden benderboard. The attractive mow strip shown here is constructed by building a simple benderboard form, filling it with concrete, and finishing it with a fitted-block motif. Mow strips for an entire front yard can be completed in a single weekend. Follow these steps for best results:

2 Fill the form with concrete to the desired depth. Float the top surface smooth, and use a curved finishing tool to strike each edge from the form.

1 Excavate a trench 6–8 in. (15–20 cm) deep and 8 in. (20 cm) wide. Using flexible benderboard, build 6-in.-wide (15-cm) side forms, drive stakes at bends and nail the boards to them. Blocks keep the form spaced correctly.

3 Allow the concrete to set. Water of formation will emerge, then begin to be absorbed; at this point, use the float to score random-length "block junctions" into the stiff cement.

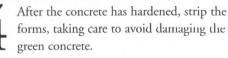

4 After the concrete has hardened, strip the forms, taking care to avoid damaging the green concrete.

INCORPORATING AMENDMENTS

Improving lawn soil—and most all lawn soil can stand some improving—assures that your lawn will thrive. There is no better opportunity to thoroughly till and amend your soil than when an old lawn has been removed.

The soil test you conducted when preparing for planting will indicate the types of amendments your soil needs. If your soil's pH balance needs adjusting to hit the slightly acidic 6.5–7.0 level a lawn requires, this is the time to incorporate either limestone to "sweeten" the soil—make it more alkaline—or sulfur to "sour" the soil—or make it more acidic. Peat moss also can acidify soil as well as improve its texture. If your soil analysis indicates that your soil is low in essential nitrogen, phosphorus, or potassium, add those fertilizers now. Compost or organic amendments improve soil quality and are generally beneficial.

Incorporating amendments is a fairly simple though precise process [see opposite]. The amounts you need depend on the area of your lawn. Most amendments are measured in terms of quantity per 1,000 square feet (93 m²) of lawn. To determine the size of your lawn, draw a rough sketch of its shape, then measure its length and width in feet (or meters), noting the distances. Then multiply the length times the width to determine the area in square feet (m²).

Compost should be applied at a thickness of about an inch (25 mm) for good loam soil, or 2 inches (50 mm) for soil that is either too sandy or too heavy. Three cubic yards (2.3 m³) of compost yield a 1-inch (25-mm) layer over 1,000 square feet (93 m²) of ground. If you are adding limestone to raise a pH level by 1.0—say from 5.5 to 6.5—you will need 28 pounds (13 kg) of lime for sandy soil but 106 pounds (48 kg) for claylike soil. If you are acidifying the soil with sulfur, a 1.0 change in pH—from 7.5 to 6.5—requires 11 pounds (5 kg) for sandy soil and 23 pounds (6 kg) for claylike soil. These percentages are available on most packages, but if not, consult with your local agricultural extension office.

Once your lawn's soil bed is prepared, you're ready to start the planting process.

Mechanical tillers are available in a variety of sizes and designs for jobs ranging from simple cultivation to complete yard renovation. Large jobs are best suited to rear-tine designs, since their heavy weight and self-propelled wheels reduce the effort required to perform the work.

APPLYING AND INCORPORATING AMENDMENTS

Amendments include agents to improve soil texture, change its pH (acid-alkaline balance), and add nutrients that are naturally deficient in the soil. Add amendments whenever you plant or restore a lawn. Spreading and tilling amendments into a lawn bed requires strength and effort. Obtain help if the task is beyond your abilities. The complete process of amending lawn soil includes the following steps:

1 Spread the amendments evenly across the area to be worked at the rate recommended on the package.

2 Make the first passes with the tiller in a sequence of parallel runs. Overlap each run by about one-third.

3 When the first passes are finished, turn and make a second series of runs at right angles to the first. This ensures that the amendments are thoroughly mixed into the soil and allows the tiller to cultivate areas that were missed the first time.

4 Tillers frequently turn up stones, leftover building materials, and other debris. Rake and remove them. Level hummocks and low spots, then rake the surface completely flat and smooth.

LANDSCAPE FABRICS

Rare is the gardener who actually enjoys pulling out weeds and other unwanted plants that have sprouted here, there, and everywhere from a groundcover bed. The quality of your gardening life will be much improved if you lay down one of the effective, low-cost weed-barrier mats or landscape fabrics on your planting bed before you install groundcover. If placed properly, these fabrics can help prevent weed growth for a number of years—and your knees will thank you for it.

Landscape fabrics typically are either woven, nonwoven, or spun-bonded synthetics that act as a barrier to germinating weeds. In the past, the same job often was done with solid plastic, which kept weeds down but also prevented water and fertilizers from getting to the plants' roots. In very wet weather, plastic could keep too much moisture in the soil at root level, promoting fungal disease. These fabrics are designed to breathe, allowing in water and air while still blocking the ability of weeds to grow.

Of the landscape fabrics available, look for those with the smallest pore size, which you can determine simply by holding up the fabric to the light. To install the weed barrier, first clear the planting area completely of weeds. Prepare your soil as you would for any planting [see opposite]. Then make a series of small, X-shaped cuts in the fabric, using sharp embroidery or other small scissors, at regularly spaced intervals. Make the cuts once the fabric is in place on the soil, keeping in mind that the larger the cut, the more likely a weed can work its way through.

Lay down the roll of fabric in parallel swaths, overlapping the edges by 6 inches (15 cm). Anchor the fabric with metal or plastic pins. Carefully work the rootball of each groundcover plug through a cut and into the soil below, tamping gently with your fingers to firm the plug in the soil. Bring the landscape fabric as tightly around the groundcover as possible and immediately water in the plantings to help them get started.

While waiting for your groundcover plugs to grow together and form a uniform bed, consider covering the fabric with an inch (25 mm) of organic mulch, such as shredded bark, to camouflage the fabric, hold in moisture, and further discourage weed growth.

Install a porous plastic barrier fabric beneath your groundcovers to block light and prevent germination of unwanted weeds.

INSTALLING A WEED BARRIER

Nearly all groundcovers benefit from the installation of a weed barrier beneath the soil surface. In the past, impermeable plastic was used, but porous barrier fabrics not only have the advantage of blocking weed growth by preventing germination of seed but of allowing water to pass through them to the ground below, preventing excessive runoff and making irrigation more efficient. Follow these easy steps to install weed-barrier fabric beneath the groundcover in your yard:

1 Prepare the soil, incorporating abundant organic compost into it and raking the bed smooth and level. Sprinkle the entire bed with a balanced fertilizer according to package instructions.

2 Lay down weed-barrier fabric, overlapping each course 6–8 in. (15–20 cm). Weight it with stones during installation, then fasten it to the soil with wire or plastic stakes.

3 Spread planting mix over the weed barrier in a layer 1–2 in. (25–50 mm) thick. Rake it to an even covering.

4 With your hands, dig down to the weed barrier and cut X-shaped holes. Plant the groundcover through the holes and press them firm.

P lanting a new lawn requires effort and commitment. Depending on its size and whether you need to take out an old lawn first, the process can take anywhere between a month and several months from start to finish. Done right, however, your efforts will be rewarded for years to come.

If you need to remove an old lawn, you first must kill it, either by smothering it with newspapers or plastic covering if it is small, by tilling it, or by employing grass-killing chemicals (sodium glyphosate), which require a week or more to take effect.

You should check the grading of the site—a lawn should slope slightly away from your home's foundation. If swampiness, puddling, or flooding has been a problem in the past, you may need to install drainage systems. If you have a deeply sloping site, you may want to have it engineered first.

Once your plot is graded, tilling will be needed to break up any compaction and allow you to fully amend the soil with any texture agents, pH adjusters, or fertilizers, as indicated by your soil test results.

Only now are you truly ready to plant, which is the subject of this chapter. In the following pages, you will learn how to level and rake, roll and topcoat, in preparation for planting your lawn, either with seed, sprigs, or plugs or by laying rolled sod.

Putting in a new lawn clearly takes some effort and planning, and it's a project best done only if you have sufficient time to complete it correctly. The more diligent the work upfront, however, the better the results. Be honest with yourself about the time and energy you can put toward it, and include helpers or tradesmen in your plans if necessary. Lawns are a dominant feature of most yards, which makes them worth doing right.

Preparation— from leveling and raking to rolling and topcoating— are the keys to a successful new lawn

Planting a New Lawn

A beautiful autumn scene, with a weed-free, well-maintained lawn belies the steps taken to prepare the soil, plant the lawn, and care for it.

LEVELING AND RAKING

Lawns grow and look their best when the ground beneath them is level. Gently rolling undulations work well when you're dealing with large areas, but in the average suburban setting, flatter is better.

Going to the effort to level your lawn is not merely an aesthetic decision, however. An uneven lawn surface is not simply unattractive, it's trouble in the making. High spots will dry out because water sheds from them before it can be absorbed. Low spots will puddle and become a breeding ground for fungal disease. Grass roots may have difficulty taking hold.

If your land is flat as a table, you're in luck. All you need do is make sure the lawn slopes slightly away from the house foundation—1–2 feet (30–60 cm) of drop per 100 feet (30 m) if the lawn goes right up to the foundation. The entire area should be raked smooth of dirt clods, twigs, and leaves.

Most gardeners, however, must deal with the lumps and bumps of typical garden terrain. If the bumps are relatively minor, you can fill them with fresh topsoil—but resist the temptation to rake topsoil from a higher spot to fill in or you will rob that area of good soil.

If the lumps and bumps are significant or the slope too steep, consider regrading the property. If the area is moderately sized, you can do it yourself—you'll need a wheelbarrow and shovel, a spirit level, a long-handled steel rake, and a little time and patience.

Checking the level of your lawn can be done in several different ways. For smaller areas, buy about a dozen 1×1-inch (25×25-mm) wood stakes and paint a line around each 5–6 inches (13–15 cm) from the top. Establish the level [see opposite] that you want the lawn to be and insert one of the pegs so that the mark is aligned with the future soil surface.

Position a second peg about 6 feet (1.8 m) away. Use the spirit level to adjust the height of the second peg until its mark is level with the first. Now, add or take away soil until the the surface is even with the marks on both pegs. Continue to insert pegs at 6-foot (1.8-m) intervals and rake the soil to create a level surface.

Even smaller areas can be leveled using a straight board, a carpenter's level and four pegs. Insert the pegs into the soil, two at each end of the area to be leveled, rest the board atop them, then adjust them until the board is level. Proceed as before, raking and filling until the area is level.

To prepare your lawn bed, rake it smooth. Use a wide rake and dispose of all pebbles, rocks, debris, dirt clods, twigs, leaves, and anything else that isn't finely ground soil. These innocent-looking troublemakers can impede the uniform growth of seed or sod more than you can imagine.

To level your soil surface, you'll need a shovel and wheelbarrow, a level—and a good long-handled steel rake.

CONSTRUCTING AND USING A SPIRIT LEVEL

Leveling a large area without sophisticated transits or laser equipment can be done easily and simply, using either a line level mounted on a string between two stakes or with a simple spirit level constructed from a garden hose, clear aquarium vinyl tubing, and a few fittings. Since water naturally seeks its own level, a spirit level instantly establishes an absolutely level plane from which the ground surface below can be measured. It is a quick and easy way to establish a single reference point when leveling a large area. Follow these instructions to construct and use a spirit level:

2 Fill the entire hose with water, taking care to prevent any air bubbles from forming. The water should appear in the clear vinyl tube at each end.

1 Attach a PVC hose-bib connector to a thread-to-slip PVC coupler, then 18-in.-long (45-cm) clear vinyl tube. Use vinyl glue to waterproof the connection. Make two fittings and attach to a hose.

3 With a helper, position one end of the hose at the first reference point, a place to which you wish to compare the level of other locations. Measure the distance from the water surface in the tube to the ground below.

4 Position the other end of the hose at the point of comparison. Measure the distance to the soil surface. The different measures between the two points reflects the difference in level across the distance being spanned.

ROLLING AND TOPCOATING

Once you've leveled and raked a lawn bed, you may be tempted to proceed directly to installing the lawn itself; if you do, you'll probably regret it. If you've machine tilled your soil, simply leveling and raking it smooth does not guarantee a flat, smooth lawn surface, no matter how it looks.

In addition to incorporating amendments—any pH adjusters such as lime or sulfur, and any of the major nutrients (nitrogen, phosphorous, or potassium) to ensure your soil will nurture the type of lawn you've chosen—tilling also incorporates a good deal of air below the soil's surface. If you install a new lawn at this point, the first watering will cause the soil to settle into the air pockets, potentially leaving you with a lumpy, bumpy lawn.

Aside from wreaking havoc with your croquet game, this bumpiness can be a particular problem if you've seeded your lawn, since the seeds will wash down from the high spots and settle into the low spots, creating a patchy growth pattern. If you have put down sod, an uneven lawn surface may cause the sod to lose contact with the soil surface in spots. Without that contact, sod in those areas almost surely will dry up, turn brown, and die.

To ensure a compact, flat lawn, roll the lawn bed with a water-filled roller after leveling and raking. Roll as you would mow, in one direction, up and back, then roll perpendicular to your original direction, in a cross-hatch pattern. After rolling, take a good hard look at the bed. Fill in any low spots with extra soil and roll over these spots again to compact them firmly.

For extra insurance, you may want to topcoat the lawn bed as well. Topcoating involves spreading a thin layer of subsurface mulch, no deeper than one inch (25 mm), across the top of the bed and leveling it out until it is dispersed uniformly. The mulch can be plain sand (used for most putting greens), which will yield the flattest surface. The mulch also can be a mix similar to potting soil, composed of organic material mixed with sand. Once you've laid down the mulch and raked it smooth and level with the back of a rake head, roll it firm.

Think of rolling and topcoating as a welcoming committee for your new lawn, encouraging it to stay awhile.

1 Using either a front- or rear-tine tiller, make two passes across the area to be planted, one perpendicular to the other, thoroughly mixing the soil to a depth of at least 16 in. (40 cm).

PREPARING SOIL

The secret to a successful lawn installation is thorough preparation of the soil before the site is seeded. Proper preparation requires some effort and strength but simple skills. Soil for planting either turfgrass or groundcover should be tilled at least 16 in. (40 cm) deep. If the soil is dense with clay or too sandy and loose, amend it with compost to add organic matter and improve its texture. For very claylike soils, add gypsum. Follow these easy steps when preparing your soil for planting:

3 A water roller is available from most equipment-rental yards. Fill it with water and roll the surface. Where the soil compacts and becomes unlevel, fill it with excess soil taken from the high spots.

2 Using a fine-tined rake, rake and level the area, removing rocks, debris, roots, and any large clods.

5 Roll the surface again until the area is completely and perfectly smooth and flat. It's now ready to plant turfgrass or groundcover.

4 Spread a ½-in.-thick (12-mm) coating of planting mulch on the rolled surface.

SEEDING TURFGRASS

With your lawn bed amended, leveled, raked, rolled, and topcoated, you're now ready for the main event: seeding. Seeding, of course, is only one method of planting turfgrass. In fact, not all turfgrasses can be planted from seed. Many warm-season grasses, such as St. Augustine grass, can be planted only with plugs or sod. Conversely, some varieties of turfgrass are unavailable as sod, and can be purchased only as seed. This is particularly true if you want a mixture of grasses. While seeding requires some work, vigilance, and patience, it's far cheaper than the other methods. Best of all, a seeded lawn tends to be a very sturdy lawn because it grows by rooting itself firmly into the seed bed.

The amount of seed you'll need depends on the type of turfgrass and will be indicated on the package, likely in pounds (kg) per 1,000 square feet (93 m²).

Sow warm-season grasses in spring and cool-season grasses in late summer or early autumn, depending on your climate zone. Before you start seeding, make sure there is no wind and the soil has been moistened to a depth of about 6 inches (15 cm) several days before. Seeding a lawn can be downright fun. You can do it by hand, but if you suspect at all that you're not getting even coverage, you may want to opt for a more predictable method—a drop spreader or a cyclone seeder, both of which are available for rental.

Drop spreaders are like fertilizer or mulch dispensers—they drop seed as you push the seeder along in lines equal to the width of the seeder. Adding some vermiculite into the mix can help spread the seed better. Whirligig or cyclone seeders spew seeds in a circular pattern and generally are a less precise method. With either type, make two passes at right angles to ensure good coverage.

After the seed is dispensed, rake the seeds lightly into the top ⅛ inch (3 mm) of soil and smooth out the surface. A long-tined leaf rake is perfect for both jobs, first with the prongs down to rake in the seed, then flipped on its back to smooth the soil. You may want to dispense a light layer of lawn-starter fertilizer over the top and possibly some peat moss as a mulch over that to a depth of ⅛–¼ inch (3–6 mm). Roll the surface to ensure the seed has a solid footing in the soil. Now, you need to water, but do so very carefully—this step is make-or-break for your newly seeded lawn. Too much water applied with too much force will cause your evenly distributed seeds to flow together in rivulets or congregate around tiny pods of water. You want complete control

Large areas of turf should be seeded with a drop spreader. The spreader's flow adjustment should be set to deliver seed evenly at the rate recommended by the supplier.

over your watering, so do it by hand with a hose. Get the finest-spray hose-end nozzle you can find and lightly water your lawn daily, sometimes twice daily, keeping it moist until your seeds germinate, sprout, and emerge from the soil. Germination times vary by grass type, but your lawn should be up sometime between a week and three weeks.

You will save yourself heartache if you take the time to cordon off your newly planted area with cord tied with bright cloth flags to stave off two-legged and four-legged intruders. If you have a particularly active child or rambunctious dog, low plastic fencing might be a wise choice.

Finally, what do you do about birds? They will love you for providing them with such easy meals, and there's not a whole lot you can do to drive them off. Covering your lawn is simply not practical. Some people suggest stringing a spider's web of cord around and across to discourage them, shooing them, or spraying them with water, but these methods provide little deterrent. The truth is, birds will eat your seed. Trust that you've sown enough seed to yield a handsome lawn and keep the local birds fat and happy at the same time.

There is an alternative to seeding by hand or machine. Hydroseeding is a one-step process employed by commercial landscaping companies to "blow" a mix of grass seed, fertilizer, fiber mulch, and water onto a seed bed. The mulch protects the seed from drying out, the fertilizer gives it a quick start, and the results generally are good. If you are trying to cover difficult slopes, hydroseeding is a good option.

SEEDING A LAWN

Seeding can be done as soon as the soil is tilled, raked, leveled, and rolled. Use a rotary hand spreader for small to midsize areas following the steps shown here:

1 Fill the spreader with seed and adjust the flow-rate control as recommended on the seed package. Make two passes over the area, the second at a right angle to the first to ensure even coverage.

2 After seeding, roll the seed into the soil surface to ensure good contact. Topcoat with ¼ in. (6 mm) of mulch and roll again.

3 Gently water the planted seed using a misting nozzle. Saturate the soil and keep it constantly moist for the first 10 days, or until germination.

INSTALLING TURF

If your time is valuable, or if you simply want instant results, installing rolled turf, or sod, is the fastest means to a new lawn. Sod is adult grass, grown at turf farms, carefully sliced with a sod cutter below the root zone in strips 6–8 feet (2–2.5 m) long, 2 feet (60 cm) wide, and 1–3 inches (25–80 mm) thick, depending on the type of grass and sod farm's equipment. The strips are either rolled or folded for installation. Sod is cut to order; place your request with at least a week's lead time.

Sod installation is not for procrastinators. You order the amount of sod you need, usually in increments of 100 square feet (9 m²) plus about 10 percent extra, and it shows up the day you have set aside to plant it. Sod should be installed immediately—it generates heat when rolled or folded and can start dying within a day, especially in warm weather, and if it is not kept sufficiently moist. Certainly within two days it will begin to deteriorate significantly. The point is, with sod, you need to pick a day for installation and commit to it 100 percent or you risk losing a sizable investment.

You will be limited in your turfgrass selection when you order sod. Most sod consists of a single species, or a blend of cultivars, rather than a blend of grasses. This means it is more prone to disease. Since you've got a lot at stake, purchase only certified product from a recommended sod supplier. Sod farms are not that easy to find, particularly if you live in an urban area, so rely on your local garden center for ordering. Your local agricultural extension office also might be able to help in the search. A reputable sod farm will take back or make good on problem strips.

When the sod arrives, examine samples for weedy grasses, any signs of disease or bugs, and any grass type different from what you ordered. Reject pieces that are yellowed or bluish-green, have holes or tears in them, fall apart as you pick them up, or are too dry. If you find these problems with a number of strips, reject the lot.

With your ground prepared for planting—tilled, amended, leveled, raked, topcoated, and rolled—you're set to go. Several days before planting day, water the soil thoroughly. You want to install sod onto moist, but not wet, soil. Make sure the turf arrives either early in the day or the night before planting. Then, get up with the crows to tackle the job. Bring a thin sheet of plywood to kneel on as you go, to avoid trampling the turf, and a sharp sod knife to cut the sod.

After the laying is completed [see opposite], thoroughly soak the lawn to a depth of 6 inches (15 cm) or more. For about two weeks, water the sod at least twice daily, morning and late afternoon, and maybe midday as well if the weather is hot and dry. Keep foot traffic light. The sod will soon establish itself.

Sod can dry out quickly, so if possible have it delivered early in the morning on the day it is to be installed and certainly no earlier than the evening before.

ROLLED-TURF INSTALLATION

Rolled turf is popular in nearly every geographic region because of its simplicity and the near certainty of a good result. Turfgrass is grown at a sod farm, under ideal conditions, then is cut from the soil and rolled for delivery to the planting site, usually on the day of planting. Turf requires good soil contact and heavy watering for the first two weeks, until the grass roots become established in their new home. Prepare the soil as for seeding, by tilling, amending, raking, leveling, and rolling. Then install the rolled turf as shown:

1 Laying the starter row is the most important step in installation. Make sure that it is perpendicular to sidewalks or mow strips to avoid excess cutting.

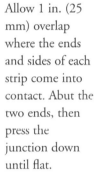

2 Allow 1 in. (25 mm) overlap where the ends and sides of each strip come into contact. Abut the two ends, then press the junction down until flat.

4 Make junctions in a laid-on-laid brick pattern, avoiding runs of adjoining joints. After the turf is placed, water it thoroughly and daily thereafter for the first 10 days.

3 Use a pruning or turf saw to trim as necessary to fit the rolled turf around mow strips, sidewalks, planters, and the like. Cut carefully to avoid damage to the turf.

PLUGGING SOUTHERN GRASSES

Another method of planting southern grasses is by installing plugs of turf. Plugs are 2- to 4-inch (5–10 cm) circular or square chunks of sod that are planted at regular intervals from one another. The upside of planting plugs is that it is cheaper than laying sod, and it gives you a mature lawn faster than sowing seed. The downside is that installation is time and labor intensive, and it will take time to achieve even coverage. The gaps between the plugs also are prey to weed infestation before the lawn fills in.

Plugs usually come precut; to save money, you can buy sod and cut your own plugs with a steel plugger. Some grasses also come in trays of plugs, which tend to have well-formed root structures encased in soil. These suffer less trauma at transplanting than plugs cut from sod. Whatever your choice, avoid buying your stock until your soil is perfectly prepared for planting [see Preparing Soil, pg. 43].

Planting plugs is a little like planting flowering bulbs except that you plant in spring rather than in autumn. Begin the planting as early in the morning as you can, preferably on a cool, overcast day. Keep your sod or plugs in the shade under a damp cloth or towel. If you're cutting your own plugs, cut only enough for a row or two at a time. As you press each plug into its hole, give it a good dousing of water to keep it hydrated until the final watering.

Once you have installed all of the plugs, water the entire area thoroughly. Because so much of the lawn area is still bare ground, water frequently, sometimes several times a day in hot, dry weather. It is critical that you avoid letting the soil surface dry out until the plugs become established. One watering should be done late at night to maximize the amount of time the water has to penetrate without evaporation. Mulching also will help the ground retain moisture until the plugs grow and fill in. When the plugs begin to grow, fertilize every six to eight weeks to encourage spread. Hold off mowing until the plugs are thoroughly established.

The types of southern, warm-season grasses that take best to plug planting include St. Augustine grass, which should be spaced 6–12 inches (15–30 cm) apart; Bermuda grass, which should be set 12 inches (30 cm) apart; and centipede grass and zoysia, both of which should be placed 6 inches (15 cm) apart because they grow more slowly. To plant 1,000 square feet (93 m²), you need 30–50 square feet (3–5 m²) of St. Augustine grass or Bermuda grass and 100–150 square feet (9–14 m²) of centipede grass or zoysia.

If you're planting a large lawn on a budget, you can't find a thriftier method than planting with plugs.

Where soil has a good workable texture, a mini-tiller is sufficient to prepare the soil for installing seed, turf, plugs, or sprigs.

INSTALLING PLUGS

1 Follow the plug supplier's recommendation for spacing the turfgrass or groundcover. Using a tape measure, lay out a string grid across the area. Each junction marks the site of a plug.

Turfgrass for southern lawns is sometimes sold in plugs—small colonies of grass—that are installed in a grid and allowed to spread out and fill the lawn area. Such grasses expand by sending out shoots, called rhizomes, which root in nearby soil. The key to a successful installation is spacing the plugs correctly and evenly throughout the area being planted. A few minutes taken to lay out the bed pays big dividends when the job is finished. Follow these steps to plug your southern grasses:

2 Dig a planting hole beneath each junction in the string, and plant a plug at its center.

3 Use a tamping tool to press each plug into good soil contact, then water the bed. As for rolled turf, water heavily the first 10 days.

INSTALLING SPRIGS

$\mathcal{S}$ome colonizing turfgrass species are sold as sprigs. Each sprig is a complete plant, with leaf blades and roots. They are sprinkled across the area to be planted, rolled into good soil contact, then watered and allowed to root. In a few months, they begin sending out runners and filling in the lawn. Start by preparing the soil for planting—tilling, amending, raking, leveling, and rolling. Follow the easy steps shown:

1 Each sprig is a complete grass plant. Scatter them densely across the area to be planted so that each sprig is no more than 2 in. (5 cm) away from its nearest neighbor.

2 As an area is completely sprigged, use a shovel to scatter a thin layer of topcoat mulch, about ¼ in. (6 mm) thick.

3 Roll the topcoat and the sprigs into good soil contact. This allows the plants to become established more quickly than if left loose.

4 Using a fine-spray nozzle, water the sprigs and soil until the water has penetrated to a depth of at least 2 in. (5 cm). Keep the sprigs constantly moist for the first two weeks after they are planted.

Mowing is like pruning—it encourages the grass blades to spread out and fill in, creating the uniform, dense carpet that we all know and love. If you mow a new lawn too soon, however, you risk pulling up newly laid sod or pulling out the young seedlings that have yet to establish a strong foothold in the lawn bed.

MOWING FOR THE FIRST TIME

Whether you've planted your lawn using seed, sprigs, plugs, or sod, wait until the blades have grown to be 4–5 inches (10–12 cm) tall before mowing. Sod should not be touched for ten days to two weeks after installation and should show signs of vigorous growth before being mowed.

When mowing a new lawn, remove a small amount of blade the first time around—just enough to tidy up the lawn's appearance and encourage the turf to spread but not enough to strip away the seedlings' capacity to photosynthesize. As with all lawns, new or old, make sure the grass is dry when you mow. Also, avoid making any sharp turns or abrupt starts and stops, which can tear up new turf. The most important factor is the type of mower you use.

For first-time mowing, the best choice is a reel mower, preferably hand rather than gas powered. A hand-powered reel mower features curved blades that spin around a fixed-bed knife, cutting the lawn with a scissorlike snipping action, producing a clean cut across the top of the grass blade. A rotary mower has a rotating blade that sits parallel to the lawn surface and whips across it. Dull blades tear the grass more than cut it. After your lawn is well established, you can use a rotary mower, but for this first time, use a reel mower. Also, don't worry about picking up the clippings—they will decompose quickly and provide a nitrogen boost to your new lawn.

After your first mowing, water the lawn well. Turfgrass goes into mild shock after mowing, and watering will help your new lawn regain its food-synthesizing capacity.

(Top) Whether you've planted your lawn from sod, seed, sprigs, or plugs, wait until it is 3–4 inches (8–10 cm) in height before mowing for the first time. Make the first run in a series of parallel passes. (Left) Turn and make a second run at right angles.

INSTALLING GROUNDCOVERS

Installing a low-growing, perennial groundcover is not that different from installing plugs of southern turfgrass. Low groundcovers, such as dichondra, moss, chamomile, ivy, creeping thyme, and the like are hardy turfgrass substitutes that can take some foot traffic, particularly when planted among paving stones and walkways. Some, dichondra and moss in particular, make wonderful small-space lawns, although they can require regular maintenance. Low groundcovers often are available in economical bedding flats that you will need to cut apart to form uniform planting colonies. Planted in the ground at regular intervals, the groundcover plants grow together and spread, ultimately connecting to create a seamless mass planting.

Some groundcovers, such as ivy, are easily distinguishable individual plants and can be set in the soil the same way you would flowers in a bed. Several days before planting, work 1–2 inches (25–50 mm) of compost and any other needed amendments into the top foot (30 cm) of soil [see Preparing Soil, pg. 43]. Measure out the proper distances and mark the planting bed's surface where the plants will go. Separate one plant at a time from the flat, keeping as much of its rootball intact as possible. Set flats in the shade as you plant, covering them with newspaper or plastic to retain moisture. Place each plant in its own hole, spread out the roots below ground level as you firm, and spread any runners atop the soil. Keep each plant at the same height as it was in the flat, keeping the crown, or the junction of root and stem, at surface level. When all the plants are in, water them well and keep the soil evenly moist until they take hold and start to grow together. Groundcover beds are prime breeding grounds for weeds so consider planting your groundcover with a landscape-fabric weed barrier [see Installing a Weed Barrier, pg. 37].

Dichondra and chamomile form dense mats of tiny plants, and it's difficult to see where one leaf stops and the other begins. These groundcovers, which generally take some foot traffic, should be planted the way you would plant plugs [see opposite]. As with any new planting, keep it well-watered until it begins to grow together and mulch in the spaces between the plant plugs. Weed barriers are less effective for these low-growing groundcovers, so be extra vigilant about removing weeds as soon as they break the surface.

Groundcovers make an ideal transition between turfgrass lawns and perennial flower borders, or they can be used as a replacement for a turfgrass lawn.

PLANTING GROUNDCOVER $\mathcal{G}$roundcovers are planted in much the same way as plugs. Spacing the plants properly is important to achieve a good result; consult the greengoods supplier or refer to the plant tag in the groundcover flat. Follow the steps shown to plant a spreading groundcover.

1 Space the plants evenly across the bed as recommended by the grower. Avoid spacing plants either too far apart or closer than recommended.

2 After the plants have been spaced, set each aside and dig a planting hole. Set the plant into the hole.

3 Press the plant's roots down with both hands to ensure good contact with the soil. This is essential if the plant is to root quickly.

4 Gently water after each planting. Keep the soil continuously moist for the first week, then reduce the frequency.

R enovation, or restoring your existing lawn, is the process of curing your lawn's current ills and reseeding with the same or a different type of turfgrass to improve its health and overall appearance. Secondary goals may be to increase its tolerance to traffic, shade, or drought. Investigating the various problems that caused your lawn to get to an ill-kempt state in the first place can take time, but it's worth the effort. Starting a lawn from scratch is an expensive, involved procedure. If your grading, soil quality, and soil density generally are good, and your existing lawn is mostly disease and weed free, you're better off saving your lawn.

In the pages to come, we'll take you through the process of investigating and diagnosing your current lawn's problems as preparation for renewed life. We start with how to assess your soil and site with an eye to improving the lawn's general condition. These inquiries include spotting site-related problems such as low spots in the lawn, inadequate in-ground irrigation, lack of clear-cut borders between lawn and flower beds, as well as the soil's ability, or inability, to support the lawn properly. We'll show you how to test for your soil's drainage capacity, how to spot broadleaf and weedy grasses that have invaded your lawn, and how to diagnose and treat the causes of all those dead patches—fungus, disease, pests, or your dog's personal habits. Once you've diagnosed the trouble, we'll tell you how to treat these conditions.

Finally, while we can't tell you how to retrain Rover, we'll give you some tips on how to mitigate the damage he can inflict on your long-suffering lawn.

> Renovating a lawn includes diagnosing its condition and taking steps to correct its ills and treat its illnesses

Renovating an Existing Lawn

Dead patches can be caused by any number of maladies, including pests, fungus—even a pet's personal habits. Identifying the cause is the key to treating the problem effectively.

ELIMINATING BROADLEAF WEEDS

Broadleaf weeds—dicots that emerge with two seed leaves—are easy to spot in a lawn. They look like small plants and often send up flowers destined to spread seeds across the lawn. Broadleaf weeds include such plants as dandelions, clover, creeping Charlie (also known as moneywort), knotweed, oxalis, plantain, purslane, curly dock, mallow, spurge, chickweed, henbit, yarrow, and thistle. Some are perennial, while the others are mainly summer annuals, germinating in spring and maturing in autumn, producing seed as they go. They are a bane to lawn perfectionists and rapidly spread unless eliminated early.

If the offending plants are small and few, you might want to take care of the problem the old-fashioned way—dig them out with a weeding fork or other weeding tool. Make sure to get the taproot, however, since otherwise they will regenerate quickly.

If the problem already is widespread, you may want to resort to herbicides. Choose postemergent herbicides as opposed to preemergent herbicides, which work better on grassy weeds, or monocots. Postemergent herbicides kill weeds once they are growing and are designed to kill broadleaf plants without damaging turfgrass. As with all herbicides, use them very carefully. Your annuals, perennials, shrubs, and trees also are broadleaf dicots and will die along with your broadleaf weeds if you do not follow the package instructions for use exactly. In fact, for broadleaf weeds growing near planting beds and trees, be safe and use a garden spade for removal.

Postemergent herbicides primarily are absorbed through the leaves, so opt for liquid sprays rather than dry granular types if possible. The chemicals frequently are mixed with water in a sprayer attached to a garden hose, but use care—the higher the water pressure the more likely the solution is to carry over to your other plants. Apply herbicides during the growing season, either early spring or late summer to early autumn, when the temperature is 65–80°F (18–27°C). Pick a day with absolutely no wind and no rain in the forecast for at least 48 hours. The soil should be moist but not wet. You may need to repeat the application in 20 to 30 days for total control.

The best way to beat broadleaf weeds is by maintaining a thick, healthy lawn. Crab-grass seeds, for example, will not germinate as readily in low light, so raising your mowing height will cut down on light. Also practice vigilance. That adorable little dandelion soon will be joined by a legion of others if you let it propagate and go to seed.

If your weed problems are minor and you detect them early, the safest means of eradication is the good old-fashioned weed fork.

Postemergent herbicides kill broadleaf weeds—or dicots— without damaging grass. Remember, however, that your annuals, perennials, shrubs, and trees are dicots, so take great care to localize the application.

APPLYING BROADLEAF-WEED CONTROL

Most objectionable weeds are broadleaf plants, not grasses. Because they differ genetically from grasses, chemical poisons have been developed that kill the weeds without harming the turfgrass. Remember that all herbicides are powerful chemicals, so wear protective equipment when applying them, including gloves, eye protection, and a respirator. Always mix, apply, and dispose of unused chemical controls in strict accordance with their package label instructions to avoid hazard to you or the environment. Follow these steps when treating your lawn:

2 Fill an adjustable-flow, hose-end sprayer with herbicide concentrate, setting the flow rate as indicated on the package.

1 Identify the broadleaf weed and use a control that specifically lists that species. Always follow the package directions exactly.

4 In 7–10 days, the broadleaf weeds will begin to exhibit signs of necrosis and will shortly die. Rake dead weeds out of the lawn.

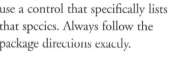

3 Spray only the weeds. Always apply controls on wind-free days, and withhold water from the lawn for 48 hours after application. Prevent children or pets access to the lawn for at least 5 days after treatment.

ELIMINATING GRASSY WEEDS

In addition to broadleaf, or dicot, weedy plants, your lawn can become infested with unwanted grasses—monocots, which put forth a single seed leaf. Any unwanted grass can be a weed in an otherwise single-species lawn—tall fescue, for example, is a perfectly fine, sturdy turfgrass itself, but it becomes a weed in your lawn if you've planted 100 percent Bermuda. Simply put, any turfgrass that is a different color, texture, and blade width than your turfgrass planting is a weed.

To eliminate unwanted grasses, first determine what grass it is, since the type of eradication method required depends on whether the grass is annual or perennial. Annual grasses respond well to preemergent herbicides, which prevent the grass seeds from germinating. Perennial grasses can be controlled only with the use of nonselective postemergent herbicides containing sodium glyphosate. They have the unfortunate side effect of killing desirable plant life as well as undesirable grasses.

Preemergent herbicides typically are dry, granular preparations applied in early spring. They should be broadcast over the affected area about two to three weeks before the soil warms and weedy grasses germinate. That means you should know when your particular weedy grass germinates and where it is located on your lawn. This second piece of information may not be as attainable as it sounds, since you'll have to recall or take note of where the weedy grass appeared the year before it disappeared as seed into the ground. You can broadcast the herbicides with a fertilizer spreader calibrated to dispense at the recommended rate. Some experts recommend broadcasting one-half the rate in one direction and one-half at a right angle to that direction for best coverage. After broadcasting, immediately water in the herbicides. Be aware that preemergent herbicides will prevent newly seeded grasses from germinating, and they may harm fine fescues or bent grasses.

Many ready-to-use weed control products are available in garden and home stores. They are convenient for dealing with small-area situations. Apply them with the same procedures used for larger control situations.

Nonselective postemergent herbicides should be applied when the grasses are growing, the temperature is 60–80°F (16–27°C), the air is still, and there is no rain in the forecast for at least 48 hours. You may need to reapply every 20 to 30 days for complete eradication.

KILLING A WEEDY LAWN

1 An entire lawn may be treated with broad-spectrum herbicide if you plan to replace it. This assures that all plants—grass, broadleaf weeds, moss, and seeds—will be eliminated from the new planting.

APPLYING BROAD-SPECTRUM HERBICIDES

Grassy weeds must be stopped before they sprout or killed using broad-spectrum herbicides that also will kill your turfgrass. Spot application of product containing sodium glyphosate is simple, effective, and short lived in the environment. Always wear protective equipment, including gloves, a respirator, and eye protection when applying herbicides to your lawn, following these simple steps:

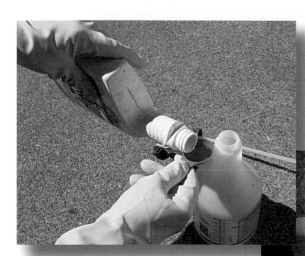

1 Spot treat unwanted grass by mixing concentrated herbicide to the package-recommended dilution for the specific grassy weed being treated.

2 Fill a hand-spray bottle with dilute herbicide and spray the unwanted weed.

3 In 7–10 days, the weed will die, exhibiting a characteristic coppery color. Reseed the area.

3 On a windless day, spray the entire area to be treated, applying the herbicide from 6–10 in. (15–25 cm) above the soil surface.

2 To treat a large area, use a pressurized tank sprayer. Measure and mix the herbicide as directed on the package and fill the tank.

4 The unwanted grass may be removed as soon as it turns copper in color.

TREATING DISEASE

Despite your best efforts, good lawns sometimes get bad diseases. Most lawn diseases are caused by fungal infections, although some, such as St. Augustine's Decline (SAD), are due to a virus. The good news about fungal infections is that proper lawn maintenance and the occasional fungicide application can eradicate them. The bad news about viruses is that they are incurable. In the case of SAD, your only alternative is to scrap the lawn entirely and replant with a disease-resistant strain.

Lawn diseases are difficult to diagnose. One day, you'll notice that something is amiss—there's a brown patch for no good reason, or some foamy white goo, or some unnaturally lush, bright green circles of growth that suddenly die. Left untreated, these fungal infections will spread to your entire lawn. Your best bet is to spot the trouble quickly, diagnose it immediately, and start treatment.

There are no all-purpose cures for fungal diseases, which is why you need to determine the specific fungus to attack it effectively. Fungus development also depends on favorable environmental conditions, which is why your first line of defense is to keep your lawn as healthy as possible. Aerating your soil, dethatching it regularly, fertilizing properly, and watering adequately but not excessively builds a better lawn that is less prone to disease.

Lawn diseases are difficult to diagnose—and some seem to happen overnight. If you wake up to this one, red thread disease, you likely will have to replace your lawn. Most fungal diseases are not so virulent, however, and may be treated.

Also, examine your own maintenance habits with a critical eye. Do you overwater? A soggy lawn is an attractive host for fungi. Are your mower blades dull? Dull mower blades leave ragged grass blades that are more susceptible to disease. Do you overfertilize? This can lead to a host of problems— most important, it can shift the pH balance of your soil to an overly acid or alkaline level that certain fungi prefer.

If you suspect your soil pH balance may be at least one of the sources of disease, try a soil test, then amend to correct the deficiency. If the soil is too acidic, which favors a disease such as brown patch, apply ground limestone to increase the pH level. If the soil is too alkaline, which fosters pythium blight, add ground sulfur as recommended on the label.

Use fungicides with caution and only as a last resort. Like nonselective postemergent herbicides, they kill the good with the bad. Your lawn needs certain beneficial fungi in the soil to promote growth. Fungicides kill the good guys, too, leaving your lawn in a generally weaker state and prone to even more disease.

Fungicides should be used only as a last resort. They do not cure fungal disease, merely prevent it from spreading. Unfortunately, they also kill beneficial fungi, leaving a lawn in a generally weaker state and prone to even more disease. Many also persist in the environment for long periods.

APPLYING GRANULAR AMENDMENTS AND FERTILIZER

Dry amendments, such as pH agents, soil looseners, and lawn fertilizers, usually are applied with a drop or broadcast spreader. The application rate is adjustable on most spreaders: set yours to one-half the package-recommended dose and apply the amendment in two passes, the second at a right angle to the first. Follow these easy steps to fertilize or apply amendments to your turfgrass lawn:

2 Make the first passes parallel to an edge, overlapping each by 5 in. (12 cm). Then make a second series of passes at right angles to the first.

1 Set the adjustable-flow rate to half the package-recommended setting for the amendment being used, then check that the release door is closed and fill the spreader. Because some spreaders leak, position it on pavement, not on turf.

3 If a second amendment or fertilizer is to be applied, reset the spreader and fill it with the second additive. Avoid mixing two amendments together for application at the same time, as coverage will be spotty.

4 Again, apply the amendment in a two-step process, assuring even coverage to the lawn. Always water in fertilizers immediately after application.

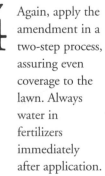

Once you have overcome the problems plaguing your lawn, by amending the soil, eliminating broadleaf weeds and weedy grasses, and treating any disease conditions, you are ready to build a healthier, even happier lawn. In this chapter, we'll take you through the basic steps to getting your lawn back into bragging condition and keeping it in shape for seasons to come.

A healthy, thriving root zone makes for a lush lawn, which means clearing away all impediments to your lawn's roots receiving the moisture, air, and nutrients they need to flourish. These maintenance practices are essential to the lawn renewal process you are undertaking now and that needs to be performed every year or two to maintain your lawn's health and vibrancy.

First comes dethatching. We'll tell you everything you need to know about thatch, that strawlike mat of undecomposed grassy material that prevents water and nutrients from reaching your turfgrass' roots. Hand in hand with dethatching is aeration, which essentially is making holes in the turf to break up compacted soil and improve the flow of oxygen to the root zone. Next we'll discuss how to topcoat and amend your soil right through the surface of your existing lawn, adding nutrients to the root zone by way of the aeration holes.

We'll also give you some tips on choosing fertilizers, and for final touchups, we'll take you through the process of reseeding those small areas where the lawn has died, either due to weed removal, compaction, or an inhospitable environment.

With all of these, we provide helpful step-by-step instructions. After you've completed these steps, you'll be amazed at the quality and vigor of your lawn.

Regular dethatching, aerating, topcoating, and amending will keep your lawn healthy and looking neat

Restoring Your Lawn

A restored lawn can return to its original vigor through simple but regular maintenance. Like any plant, all a lawn's roots require are adequate moisture, air, and nutrients.

FERTILIZING NEEDS

FERTILIZING LAWNS

1 Granular lawn fertilizer should be applied with a drop spreader. Measure the amount needed and set the flow-rate adjustment.

Turfgrass plants are hungry creatures but among the most efficient converters of nutrients to energy. Not many plants can take the regular, often severe, pruning that turfgrass does and still bounce back with such vigor and verve. Yet, turfgrass usually must have a little help to get all its needs met.

Test your soil to determine the precise methods and amounts of amendments needed to correct any deficiencies. If you find, for example, that your turf is low in the three major elements, use an all-purpose fertilizer. If your lawn is nitrogen deficient, use a fertilizer that delivers only nitrogen.

The amount of fertilizer, particularly nitrogen, you need to put down in a year is partly determined by the turf type. Apply the fertilizers consistently throughout the growing season, which also differs depending on whether the grass is a cool-season or warm-season variety. For most grasses, late spring or autumn are the best fertilizing times, although warm-season grasses require a boost from late spring through autumn and even into winter. Do not, however, fertilize cool-season grasses during midsummer.

The types of fertilizers you use and how frequently you use them are often a matter of personal philosophy. Next to pesticide use, nothing in lawn care is quite as controversial. Many gardeners swear by the simplest fertilizing techniques—leaving grass clippings on your lawn, for example, can provide one-third to one-half of your lawn's nitrogen needs for the year. Dethatching and aerating [see Dethatching, pg. 66, and Aerating, pg. 68] can do much to keep the soil's microbe populations thriving.

Ultimately, the best and most responsible fertilizing choices and techniques are the ones you make with the health of your lawn and the environment in mind.

2 Apply the fertilizer in two passes, the second at a right angle to the first, to ensure even coverage on the lawn.

3 Water immediately after fertilizing a turfgrass lawn. This dilutes the granules and distributes nutrients to the roots.

APPLYING WATER-SOLUBLE AND CONCENTRATED DRY FERTILIZER

Fertilizers are available in a wide range of forms. Two popular varieties are water-soluble and dry concentrate. Apply them following the steps shown below:

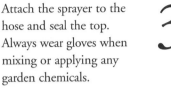

2 Attach the sprayer to the hose and seal the top. Always wear gloves when mixing or applying any garden chemicals.

3 Spray the lawn food evenly across the lawn in overlapping passes, avoiding flower beds and trees. Avoid application on windy days.

1 Apply water-soluble lawn food by filling a hose-end sprayer with the dry powder and setting the flow-rate adjustment to the package-recommended rate.

2 Set the flow-rate adjustment on the spreader to the rate recommended by the fertilizer supplier. Make two sets of passes across the lawn, the second at a right angle to the first, rotating the handle of the spreader to spray fertilizer granules.

3 Water the concentrated fertilizer into the turf, applying at least 2 in. (5 cm) of water to the lawn surface.

1 Apply concentrated granular fertilizers with a rotary handheld spreader. Fill the spreader.

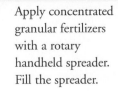

DETHATCHING

Older lawns, particularly if over the years they received quick-greening fertilizers (which tend to spur top growth without providing much root support), are likely to have developed thatch.

Thatch is the dead and dry remains of turfgrass roots, stolons, and rhizomes that don't decompose as quickly or easily as they should. Spotting thatch is easy. Take a walk across your lawn. Does it feel springy? If so, you have some thatch. Does it feel very springy, and do your feet sink deeply into the lawn? If this is the case, you've got a lot of thatch. Now get down on your hands and knees and inspect the lawn closely. You should be able to see soil between the blades. If you don't see soil, but you see instead yellow strawlike material, you have thatch. Some thatch is normal, too much is not desirable. Insert a metal ruler or tape measure into the turf until it hits soil and note the depth of the thatch only.

A little bit of thatch can be a good thing. Thatch generally is acceptable if its thickness is less than ¼ inch (6 mm). If it's between ¼ and ½ inch (6–13 mm), you're on your way to a thatch problem. If it's more than ½ inch (13 mm) thick, the problem has arrived.

Some measure of thatch helps a lawn retain moisture and can block pests from attacking grass roots. A lot of it is an indicator of a general breakdown in the decomposition process that is essential for healthy turfgrass growth. In rich, healthy soil, thatch is broken down fairly quickly by microorganisms and, most important, earthworms, who munch it up and reduce it to precious humus. Ironically, many of the commercial fertilizers, fungicides, and pesticides that get added to our lawns drive up the acidity of the soil and send earthworms and other microbes packing. Without them, thatch does not break down, pure and simple. This dynamic can be reversed by aerating and "sweetening" the soil to a 6.5–7.0 pH range and by topcoating with rich organic matter such as peat moss. This remedy, however, can be made only after you have dethatched your lawn.

To remove thatch in a smaller lawn, you can rake it out with a special long-spined tool called a "cavex." For a larger lawn, you might want to rent a power rake, also known as a "verticutter" or "vertimower." It works like a mower, but the blades run vertically rather than horizontally, cutting up the thatch as you push it along. Then you rake up the removed thatch and dispose of it.

The process of dethatching often is combined with aeration [see Aerating, pg. 68]. Finish with a healthy topcoating. These methods will help immeasurably in restoring a lagging lawn back to health.

To remove thatch in a smaller lawn, use a special long-spined rake known as a "cavex."

A little bit of thatch is a good thing. To determine if you've got a thatch problem, inspect your turf carefully. If you can see soil between the blades, you have normal thatch.

HOW TO DETHATCH

The tool of choice for dethatching a lawn is a power dethatching machine, or vertical mower. It is available for inexpensive hire in most rental yards. The machine cuts and then removes thatch buildup from between the blades of grass in your turf, placing it on the surface of the lawn where it can be raked away and removed. Although the machine is heavy, it also is self-propelled and easy to use. Follow the process shown here to dethatch most lawns in a few hours:

1 With the dethatching machine running, make a single set of passes across the lawn, allowing the machine to set the pace with its drive wheels.

2 After the machine has completed its work, rake the thatch into a pile and remove it. Thatch generally does not make good compost.

3 A second raking at a right angle to the first will remove the last of the thatch from the lawn. Remove and dispose of it.

4 Complete the process by watering the lawn thoroughly. It quickly will fill in the bare spots created by the dethatching.

AERATING

Aerating your lawn often goes hand in hand with dethatching it, but you may need to aerate even if thatch buildup is not a problem. Aeration is the process of breaking up compacted or poorly draining soil to increase the amount of air—and most important, oxygen—that reaches the roots of the turfgrass. Roots need oxygen to thrive, and the microbial life and earthworms so necessary to maintaining a healthy lawn also need air to survive. When soil becomes compacted, either from foot traffic or heavy rains, the soil particles are squeezed together and the air is pushed out. Water fails to penetrate, drainage is slowed, and fertilizers merely wash off. The lawn's roots grow shallower and shallower, and the lawn weakens and ultimately dies.

Fortunately, diagnosing a compaction problem is as easy as diagnosing thatch. Become suspicious if water stands in pools. Grab a screwdriver and take a walk around your lawn. Starting with areas that are trafficked highly or are spindly and sparse, push the screwdriver into the ground. Does it penetrate fairly easily up to the handle? If you feel the need to run for the hammer to pound it into the ground, don't bother. You've got a compaction problem, and you need to aerate your soil.

Some gardeners aerate their lawns once a year, and that's not a bad idea. Autumn is preferable, but spring is a good second choice. As with dethatching, proper aeration requires renting a special machine, this one called a "core aerator" [see opposite].

If you have a small lawn, an alternative is to buy a hand core aerator, which looks like a gnarled garden fork. You press it down into the ground with your foot, extract it, and tap out the plugs. It takes more time and energy, but it's essential for areas where a power aerator won't fit.

Core aerating is the most intensive way of breaking up your lawn bed, and it should be an annual or biennial event. On a more regular basis, you can fight compaction by spiking your lawn. Many people wear golf shoes every time they walk out on their lawn, but this practice sounds better than it actually is. True spiking takes a tool that punctures thin, long holes into the ground allowing for better drainage and increased oxygenation. Spiking tools are readily available at most home-improvement centers and are worth the investment. Regular spiking is a good short-term method for improving your soil's condition.

It may feel as though you're killing your lawn with kindness to aerate it, but appearances are deceiving. Aeration cuts holes through the matted roots and into the subsurface soil, allowing water and nutrients to penetrate through compacted soil.

HOW TO AERATE

Aeration is best performed with a specialized machine called a core aerator, available at most rental yards. The process itself takes only an hour or so for most lawns and requires little in the way of physical strength. Core aerators drive hollow metal tubes into the turf and soil, then extract plugs and deposit them on the lawn surface, where they can be reabsorbed or removed. Follow these simple steps to aerate your lawn to reduce soil compaction and improve the flow of air and nutrients to the turf.

1 Using a core aerator, make a single series of passes across every area of the turf, allowing the machine to set the pace.

2 Extracted plugs are unsightly but quickly dissolve when the lawn is watered. If you prefer, rake and remove them before applying a layer of organic mulch ½ in. (12 mm) thick.

3 Always water your lawn after aerating it. The water will penetrate deeply into the core holes, and wash the organic mulch deep into the soil.

TOPCOATING AND AMENDING

Once you've dethatched and aerated your lawn, it's time to rebuild its overall health by adding necessary nutrients to the soil. You're off to a good start if you've let all of those unsightly plugs of grass and soil, pulled up during the aeration process, stay right where they fell. They break down in a couple of weeks and return much-needed nitrogen to the soil.

Aeration holes make wonderful conduits for passing necessary nitrogen, oxygen, and other soil nutrients to the root zone. This stage is the perfect time to topcoat your lawn. You can use organic compost or a mix of fine, not chunky-style, peat moss and weed-free topsoil, with one or two parts playground sand mixed in if your soil is claylike. You can add topsoil to the compost if it is good quality and absolutely free of weeds.

At the same time, check the pH balance of your lawn's soil and apply either lime or sulfur to correct any imbalance. This also is a good time to overseed and renew a scraggly lawn, and, if desired, you can add grass seed to the topcoating before dispensing.

Spread the mix evenly over your lawn to a depth of about ¼ inch (6 mm)—a drop spreader is a fine tool for this task.

After you have coated the lawn sufficiently, lightly rake, or even sweep with a stiff broom, the topcoating into the soil surface. Brush off as much of it as possible from the leaf blades so light can penetrate and make sure the topcoating fills in all the depressions in the soil, including the aeration holes. Once this is accomplished, water in thoroughly, either by hand or with your in-ground irrigation system [see Installing an In-ground Irrigation System, pg. 30].

Combined with dethatching and aeration, topcoating is the single best thing you can do to improve the condition of your lawn's soil. The layer of topcoating, if repeated annually, will gradually build up a kind of super soil layer over the years.

Topcoating stimulates lush grass growth and the formation and rooting of rhizomes. It helps maintain soil moisture in sandy soils and root-zone drainage in heavy soils.

As you aerate from year to year, continuing to poke holes in different spots, increasing numbers of topcoating "spikes" will penetrate the soil bed, improving overall drainage, breaking up compaction, and sending needed nutrients down to the root zone.

By topcoating, you not only are renewing your lawn but also ensuring its future health.

An easy way to spread topcoating mulch on a turfgrass lawn is with a long-handled shovel. Pick up a shovelful of mulch and swing the shovel in the direction of the turf, then pull it back suddenly. The mulch will spray off of the shovel head and spread across the turf.

TOPCOATING LAWNS

1 Spread a mixture of equal parts compost, ground peat, sand, and topsoil across the lawn with a shovel or a drop spreader. The coating should be ¼ in. (6 mm) thick.

The healthiest lawns receive more than fertilizer and water: give them a complete course of organic nutrients by topcoating. Topcoating a lawn should be done annually, during an active growth period (spring and autumn for cool-season grasses, summer for warm-season grasses). Follow the steps shown for best results on your lawn:

2 Rake the topcoat mulch into the turfgrass, working it beneath the grass blades. A long-tined lawn rake is best for this step.

4 Water the lawn thoroughly, washing the topcoat mulch off of the grass and into the soil. Apply at least 2 in. (5 cm) of water, allowing it to deeply penetrate the turf.

3 Following topcoating, use a handheld rotary spreader to add extra grass seed. It will wash into the soil and fill in any bare spots.

RESEEDING SMALL AREAS

In the process of renewing your lawn, you may notice that there are certain small spots that have failed. The grass is spindly or sparse, yellowed or browned, or gone completely. Perhaps the dog has grown a bit too fond of a certain corner, and the grass has retreated in self-defense. Maybe the watering system just doesn't reach this area with enough moisture. Possibly you've discovered just where your children have established home base for the T-ball crowd. Whatever the cause, there is an easy remedy.

Reseeding small areas is a painless and inexpensive way to renovate trouble spots in your lawn. First, clip the lawn as low as possible in the dead spot or dig it out entirely. Rake the area clear of dead grass, weeds, pebbles, and leaves. If the ground is compacted, dig up some of the soil and mix it with fresh topsoil and compost. Be wary of making the patch soil extremely fertile—you may end up with exceptional growth in that spot, which will make the rest of the lawn look pale by comparison. Even if your soil in the reseeding area is not compacted, loosen it several inches (approximately 13 cm) down with a garden fork or spade. Level the soil with the surrounding lawn surface. If the reseeding area is large, you may want to roll it flat. If it's small, tamp it down with the back side of a hoe or rake. Now seed the spot with the same turfgrass as the rest of your lawn. If you are unsure what type of lawn you have, take a small chunk of sod to your lawn supply store.

Next, follow the seeding directions for seeding turfgrass [see below and opposite]. After sowing the seeds, topcoat the area, reroll or tamp down with a hoe or rake, and water gently with a fine-mist nozzle to prevent runoff. Keep the area moist until the grass is up. Withhold mowing until the new lawn reaches the right height for the variety.

MOWING AFTER RESTORATION

As with a newly seeded lawn, mowing the first time after restoration is a delicate proposition. The goal is to curb growth and encourage the blades to spread out rather than climb, but the seedlings still are too young and fragile to have developed good root systems. Mow the first time with a hand- or gas-powered reel mower [see Mowing for the First Time, pg. 51]. A hand-powered reel mower with sharp blades cuts turfgrass more cleanly and evenly than do other mowers. The reel mower features curved blades that spin around a fixed-bed knife, cutting the lawn with a scissorlike snipping action as opposed to the tearing action of rotary mowers. Allow the seedlings to grow to 3–4 inches (8–10 cm) tall, then cut no more than ¼–½ inch (6–13 mm). Leave the clippings behind to decompose and give a shot of nitrogen fertilizer to your restored lawn. Finally, water well.

Dead spots can appear in nearly any lawn—caused by fungal disease, pet damage, failed irrigation, or excessive traffic across the turf. The solution is reseeding the area that has been affected.

1 Though it seems drastic, begin by digging the dead spot out of the lawn, using a shovel. The hole should be at least 12 in. (30 cm) deep, with straight, steep sides.

REPAIRING DEAD SPOTS

Every lawn, over time, will develop dead spots. If the cause is a care issue, say a failed sprinkler, make the necessary repairs before attempting to reseed. Otherwise, follow these steps to restore your lawn to good health:

3 Tamp the soil to compact it, using a tamping tool. Add additional soil as needed to bring it level with the turf.

2 Refill the hole, using fresh topsoil. While the replacement soil should be loam with good texture, it should have the same general characteristics as that of the rest of the lawn.

4 Seed the area with a variety or mix that matches the original turfgrass of the lawn. Avoid annual varieties—they will live only one year and then die.

6 Water the planted area with a light misting spray, taking care to avoid uncovering the grass seed.

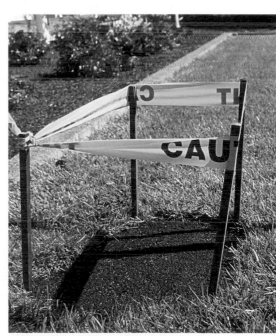

5 Lightly topcoat the seed to protect it from birds and allow it to have complete soil contact as it germinates.

7 Protect the newly repaired area with an easily seen barrier to prevent hazard from falling and to block traffic from the site.

> Maintaining a healthy lawn requires little more than proper mowing and watering techniques

Basic Lawn Care

Perhaps the greatest benefit of installing or restoring a lawn properly is that it makes care and maintenance so simple it pays back the initial hard work quickly and easily. The two critical components of good lawn care are observation and flexibility. In fact, a strict regimen is not necessarily the best way to care for turfgrass. Variables such as temperature, humidity, wind, seasonal light changes, the type of grass you are growing, and the standard of appearance you expect from your lawn all play a part in determining its care from week to week.

This chapter is all about lawn-care basics: how to provide the right amount of water for your lawn, how to evaluate the water delivery of your irrigation system, how to mow, and which type of mower to choose.

Preventing trouble and problem spotting are essential to maintaining a healthy lawn. We discuss pest and disease management, the impact of pesticides on the environment, and alternatives to their use.

If water conservation is a concern, either for resource, philosophical, or environmental reasons, you can read about xeriscaping, the art of landscaping to conserve water through proper lawn-watering methods or replacement of all or part of your lawn with water saving groundcovers.

Part of good lawn care is knowing when you need help and where to get it. In these pages, we offer advice straight from the leading lawn-care trade associations, including tips for screening and hiring the right type of lawn service. We also spotlight the many sources that provide expert help when you have specific lawn questions or when problems arise.

A careful eye and some planning are truly all your lawn-care routine requires to become a pleasurable part of gardening.

Proper mowing is the key to a healthy lawn. Mowing when the grass blades are too short or the turf is too wet are the two most commonly made mistakes.

WATERING

The watering needs of turfgrasses, more so than many other plants, vary according to a number of conditions. For example, an automatic sprinkler system does a good job of coverage but often waters too often for a lawn as it tries to meet the irrigation requirements of other shrub and tree plantings. Conversely, watering by hand usually does not provide enough uniformity or length of time to give a lawn the soaking it needs. Hose-end sprinklers can provide the soaking but rarely the uniformity. So, what do you do?

Lawns need to be watered so that moisture penetrates 6–8 inches (15–20 cm) below the soil surface. Between ½ and 1¾ inches (13–40 cm) of water will penetrate to that depth, depending on your soil type. Sandy soil allows for the fastest penetration—about 30 minutes' time—and needs only ½ inch (13 mm) of water. However, since sand dries out much faster than other soils, water needs to be provided more frequently. Clay soil retains moisture the best, but it takes more water—about 1¾ inches (40 mm)—and much more time—up to five hours—to penetrate. The ideal loam soil takes an inch (25 mm) of water and two hours' penetration time. Other soil mixes fall somewhere between these ranges.

If you have an in-ground sprinkler system, find out how long it takes it to dispense an inch (25 mm) of water across your lawn and how uniform the coverage is. To find out, set out a series of plastic cups in a grid pattern across your lawn. Turn on your sprinklers and let them run for 30 minutes. Leaving the cups in place, measure with a ruler the amount of water in them. If they have ½ inch (13 mm), you know it will take another 30 minutes to reach an inch (25 mm). If you end up with 1¾ inches (40 mm) in a few of the cups and ¼ inch (6 mm) in a number of others, you'll need to adjust your sprinkler heads to even out the flow or, possibly, add sprinkler heads to carry more water to the drier areas.

Deep, infrequent watering is the ideal irrigation method for lawns. If you are not sure of the moisture level of your soil, insert a screwdriver into the turf to check water penetration.

HOSE-END SPRINKLERS

Pulsating, Impulse, or Rotary: These shoot water out in pulsating circular or part-circular motions with paddles that break up the main stream for widespread coverage. They can be set on tripods to cover about a 100-square-foot (9 m²) area. They work well for large lawns and provide fairly uniform coverage when placed in overlapping patterns.

Whirlybird: This type works much like an overgrown in-ground sprinkler head, sending out three jets of water in a spinning pattern and depositing a lot of water quickly. It's best for small areas that don't require the unit to be moved frequently.

Stationary: Like the whirlybird, this sprinkler deposits a lot of water in a small area very quickly, so it needs to be watched carefully and moved frequently. It is inefficient for use on large areas because it does not provide even coverage.

Oscillating or Fan: These models create a rectangular pattern of water distribution but drop most of the water from above the oscillator head. Adjustable types cover between 75 and 3,600 square feet (7 m²–335 m²) but irregularly. They can be effective in small, narrow areas.

Soaker hose: Good for narrow lawn pathways and driveway grass strips, this type requires a great deal of time for a larger lawn area since it distributes water slowly through multiple pin-size holes in the hose.

TESTING IRRIGATION DISTRIBUTION

The greatest challenge for any irrigation system is to provide an evenly distributed flow of water to every area of the lawn. In-ground systems do this best, if the heads are calibrated and located correctly. Hose-end sprinklers usually leave dry spots or excessively water some areas. Measure the distribution of your sprinkler system by performing the simple test shown here:

1 Divide the lawn into a rectangular grid of 5-ft. (1.5-m) squares and place a picnic cup at each point in the grid. Turn on the in-ground sprinkler system or the hose-end sprinkler for 30 minutes.

2 After 30 minutes have elapsed, turn off the sprinklers and measure the water in each cup. All should have equal amounts of water.

3 Adjust the sprinkler heads to increase the water flow in areas that receive less water; decrease the flow for areas that receive more. Set the system timer to the duration required to deliver 1 in. (25 mm) of water. Most lawns should be watered heavily every 5–7 days.

MOWING

It may sound simplistic, but when you're planning your regular lawn-maintenance regimen, put this advice at the top of the list: mow only when the lawn needs to be mowed and water only when it needs to be watered. Good lawn care defies preprogramming, particularly mowing.

Your cool-season lawn grows at different rates at different times of the year—faster in spring and autumn, slower during the hot summer months and after fertilizing. Warm-season grasses, by contrast, grow most when the weather turns hot. While mowing once a week is almost programmed into most people's schedules, your lawn will look better and stay healthier if you mow only when the grass has reached its optimum height.

Healthy turfgrass relies on both a strong root system and sturdy blades to thrive. The surface of the grass captures the sun's rays, which in turn helps the plant photosynthesize, or produce the compounds necessary for the plant's survival. The smaller the blade, the less surface area it has to capture light and the less food it can produce to sustain a deep and thriving root system.

(Right) A rotary mower is excellent for regular cutting of turfgrass provided that it is well maintained and the blade is sharp. When the blade becomes dull or nicked (top), it mauls the grass, inviting disease and causing an unsightly appearance.

Every time you mow, your grass goes into mild to severe shock as it tries to cope with the loss of food-producing blade surface. That is why lawn experts are adamant that no more than one-third of a grass blade's height be removed with any mowing. Each turfgrass type has an ideal mowing height, from ½–3 inches (13–80 mm), depending on the variety. Allow your lawn to grow to at least ¾ inch (20 mm) in height before mowing if the ideal height of your turfgrass is ½ inch (13 mm), 4 inches (10 cm) if the ideal height is 3 inches (8 cm), and so on, using the rule that it should be half again its height.

When you mow, alter your pattern each time to keep the grass from developing a wear pattern, and never mow a wet lawn. Try to make sweeping, not abrupt, turns as you mow. Leave the grass clippings behind to decompose naturally—much of your lawn's basic nitrogen requirements will be satisfied and the need for fertilizer reduced.

Most important, keep your mower blades sharp. A dull mower will leave you with a chewed-up lawn for all your hard work; worse, it also opens the lawn to threat of disease.

Your choice of lawn mower, and your maintenance of that mower, play a big role in the overall appearance and health of your lawn.

Reel mowers, either hand or gas powered, are considered the preferred cutting tools for a lawn, though some are more expensive than rotary mowers, and you must depend on the services of a professional to sharpen the blades.

Rotary mowers, mostly gas powered but also electric, are popular for their price and for their ease of operation and maintenance. Rotary mowers, however, feature a circulating blade that sits parallel to the lawn surface and slices across the top of it, tearing the blades more than cutting them precisely, making them more prone to disease.

Many rotary mowers come with a mulching attachment that picks up clippings, chews them up, and deposits them either in a bag or on the lawn surface. You quite easily can, and should, sharpen the rotary blade with a simple file at home.

If you have a substantial lot, you may want to invest in a riding mower. The mowing deck is wider—up to 42 inches (107 cm) across—and the engine is, of course, more powerful than a powered reel or rotary mower. In terms of effort, lawn maintenance becomes a ride in the park.

A step up from the riding mower is the tractor mower, which is built to cover even more ground. These boast up to 18-horsepower engines and cut a swath as large as 48 inches (122 cm). They also feature a variety of attachments, including trailers, augers, firewood splitters, and sweepers.

Whichever type of mower you choose to buy, make sure you are comfortable with the equipment and understand thoroughly its method of operation and potential hazards before you use it.

Keeping your mower clean and its blades sharpened helps ensure a long, happy life for both the mower and your lawn.

(Top) Regular maintenance is part of lawn ownership. (Left) A classic hand-push reel mower is the right tool for small lawns. Reel mowers cleanly cut the grass rather than tear it, can be sharpened, and are simple to use.

PREVENTING WEEDS

Few garden chores are more disliked than weeding. For most turfgrasses, the best way to limit the need for weeding is to apply a preemergent herbicide, providing that your municipality permits its use. As you might deduce, preemergent herbicides are questionable, environmentally speaking. They are long-duration chemicals, taking years to leach out of the soil and even longer to degrade into harmless components. Despite these negative concerns, they are effective if used as directed, strictly in accordance with their label instructions.

Preemergent herbicides form a barrier in the soil that destroys germinating weed seeds and blocks their roots from penetrating down into the soil. They are applied in liquid or granular form, frequently in combination with fertilizers or pesticides [see bottom]. Most are applied in the spring, before soil temperatures warm and weed seeds begin to sprout.

An important consideration regarding their use is the fact that the preemergent herbicide does not recognize the difference between good seeds and bad; it blocks all seeds from germination—weed, turfgrass, flowers, and vegetables. Lawns that have been treated with preemergent herbicides may resist attempts to overseed or repair dead spots unless the treated soil is removed. Keep this drawback in mind as you set out to achieve your goal of blocking weeds. Remember that the herbicide may affect nearby plantings of trees and shrubs, as well as your lawn, and that flower beds should be protected from stray granules of the herbicide.

APPLYING A PREEMERGENT HERBICIDE

1 Fill a hand rotary spreader with herbicide, following the package label instructions.

2 Set the flow-rate setting to the recommended rate. Make overlapping passes across the lawn, covering the entire surface with herbicide.

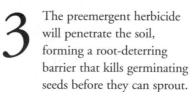

3 The preemergent herbicide will penetrate the soil, forming a root-deterring barrier that kills germinating seeds before they can sprout.

From time to time you may encounter an out-of-the-ordinary problem with your lawn—a strange brown patch that appears to grow daily. Perhaps a new lawn care product has come on the market and you want to know how safe it is to use around your pets. Maybe you're concerned about the wear resistance of your current lawn and want to know if any new, tougher types have been developed that you can use to overseed this autumn.

There are plenty of resources of all types out there, ready and willing to provide information and support. They range from the traditional—your local nursery and garden retail stores, libraries filled with reference books, and county extension offices—to electronic online sources.

If your question is basic and general, you probably can find the answer in a good old reference text. Turfgrass technology has developed faster than many other plant areas, thanks largely to the demands of the sports world. Electronic sources generally are best for finding out about up-to-the-minute developments. A number of long-time professional trade and plant associations—the Lawn Institute, the Turfgrass Information Center, and the Professional Lawn Care Association of America, to name a few—are happy to provide you with information upon request. They also can point you to local sources that can give you advice more specific to your regional area.

In general, the more specific your question is to your location and situation, the more precise and probably local your information source needs to be. For these inquiries, rely on the expertise of the staff of a local nursery as the best initial reference point. They know your area, the vagaries of the climate, how different plants perform, the common pests and diseases, and the recommended treatment. Nursery experts also know their shortcomings and usually can point you to a governmental agency that can help you find the answers if they can't. Last but not least are your local universities, many of which have agricultural extensions and public outreach for all types of gardening issues, including turfgrass and groundcover care.

OBTAINING EXPERT HELP

The array of resources for lawn inquiries is greater than ever—and more accessible than in the past. Advice from professional trade associations, governmental agencies, and university outreach programs usually is just a keystroke or page away.

PROFESSIONAL LAWN SERVICES

Without a doubt, proper lawn care takes time and effort—and the better quality your turfgrass, the more care it requires. The best way to care for your lawn is to be realistic about how much time you have to devote to it and how much a professional service can take on for you.

How do you choose a lawn-care service? A neighbor who employs one is the best source because you can see the work firsthand. Your local nursery or home garden center is another good reference source. If you use the telephone book, request references and confirm that the provider is licensed by the state for application of lawn-care products, such as pesticides. Also ask if it is a member of a trade association, such as the Professional Lawn Care Association of America (PLCAA), which offers these general guidelines for choosing a lawn-care service:

- Determine what you'd like from the service (for example, mowing, maintenance, aeration, seeding, landscaping, fertilizer and pest control applications).
- Ask for a free lawn inspection and estimate for service.
- Ask about the pricing system—which services are included in a basic fee and which, if any, are extra. Some companies work by written contract, others by verbal agreement. If you are under contract, ask whether service calls between scheduled appointments for emergencies are free or not.
- Consider paying annually instead of per visit. Often there is a discount for paying upfront for an annual contract.
- Have a complete understanding of the program before your lawn work begins. Be sure you know for what you're paying, the type and amount of treatments involved, when they will be applied, and what results can be expected.
- Find out what is, and is not, guaranteed. Some companies offer refunds if they fail to meet expectations.
- Make sure the lawn-care service is licensed for the application of lawn-care products as required by state law. You can learn what those requirements are through your state Department of Agriculture or local county extension office.
- Be sure the company is affiliated with one or more professional lawn-care associations. Most associations, such as the PLCAA, have a code of ethics and keep their membership informed about new developments in pest-control methods, safety, training, research, and regulation.
- If you are concerned about a service's business practices and track record, contact your local Better Business Bureau.

All lawn-service providers are licensed pesticide and herbicide technicians. They must comply with all local and national regulations for the mixing, care, application, and disposal of lawn chemicals.

Lawn-care services make regular visits to fertilize and evaluate the need for pesticide and herbicide applications.

Over the years, turfgrass lawns have been accused of being water guzzlers, resource hogs, or both. This reputation likely has come more from the lawn keepers than the lawns themselves, which require only thoughtful watering to survive and thrive.

XERISCAPING AND WATER CONSERVATION

Xeriscaping is the term given to water conservation, or drought-tolerant landscaping. The root "xeros" comes from the Greek word for dry, and "scaping" was borrowed from the familiar landscaping. To many who are only a little familiar with the term, xeriscaping conjures up an image of pale, bone-dry desert dirt with scraggly cactus and weedy-looking shrubs dotting an inhospitable landscape. In fact, xeriscaping simply means planting and caring for plants in a way that minimizes water use—and lawns are well included in that scope. Many turfgrasses are drought tolerant in all climate zones. Among the cool-season grasses that fall in this category is tall fescue, but not bent grass; for warm-season climates, hybrid Bermuda would be the choice, but not centipede grass.

Knowing how to water your lawn most efficiently plays a big part in water conservation. This means watering very deeply, so the water penetrates 6–8 inches (15–20 cm) below the soil surface, watering slowly so no runoff is incurred, and usually watering infrequently [see Watering, pg. 76]. It also means paying more attention to wind than to heat and checking automatic sprinkler systems to make sure they provide even coverage and do not deliver too much water (see Testing Irrigation Distribution, pg 77].

If even this amount of water use is of concern, consider putting in some groundcovers, which on average require far less water than even the least-thirsty turfgrass lawn. Since most groundcovers shade the ground, they are excellent at moisture retention and can be a colorful alternative to traditional turfgrass lawns. They also take less maintenance overall, so you gain the benefits of easier upkeep as well as the elimination of chemical-fertilizer use. Some of the best groundcovers include winter creeper, or purple-leaf winter creeper, which is resistant to the vagaries of climate, soil conditions, and rambunctious pets; cinquefoil, which works well in large areas and tolerates foot traffic; the ground-hugging creeping sedum and hens and chickens; and woolly speedwell, a type of veronica that is especially suited to high-altitude climates. In addition, planting groundcovers is a quick and simple process [see Planting Groundcovers, pg. 53].

Xeriscapes can be orderly and neat or nearly woodland wild. They rely on plants that require less water than those typical for home gardens and landscapes.

PEST AND DISEASE MANAGEMENT

Nothing is quite as controversial in the gardening world as the use of herbicides, fungicides, and pesticides. After all your hard work and sizable investment in creating a beautiful expanse of green, it's difficult to watch it become a smorgasbord for every slimy, spiny creature in the neighborhood, riddled with weeds, or turned to brown mush by an invasive disease. You want revenge, but reliance on chemicals could be a mistake.

Toxic chemicals are effective killers, no doubt. The trouble is, they are often too effective, killing beneficial microbial life and insects. Even as restricted as your use is, your lawn might begin to decline because the overall condition of the soil is poor due to a lack of earthworms. The lawn might develop excessive thatch because there are no microbes to break down the organic matter essential to your turfgrass. Ultimately, such a weakened lawn will become prey to other diseases and pests not targeted by the chemical you've used.

All of this does not even mention the unseen harms— synthetic chemicals leaching far down into the soil and aquifer to reach the groundwater that leads to your city's water supply, slow-to-degrade chemicals washing as rain or sprinkler runoff into the streets and sewers where they dump into the ocean, birds and other animals eating the poisoned bugs and depositing the residues as waste here, there, and everywhere. Evaluate what price you're willing to pay for cosmetic "perfection" in your lawn.

There are situations and reasons to employ some chemicals, but remember at all times that they are hazardous. If you decide to use a lawn chemical, read the label before you buy it and every time before you use it, following the instructions exactly.

There are, happily, alternatives to chemicals for the eradication of pests, weeds, and diseases. The principles of organic and integrated pest management (IPM) were developed for agricultural use, but they apply equally to home gardening and lawn care. IPM is based on the natural system of checks and balances to combat weeds, bugs, and diseases. The first premise is to prepare and plant properly, then maintain, a healthy, thriving lawn. If a lawn falls prey to pests or disease, or turns into a weed bed, it usually is because the soil is not healthy or the blades have been damaged—its system is out of whack from too much high-nitrogen fertilizing, not enough of the right fertilizer, too much or too little water, or too low a mowing height.

Research indicates that the micro organisms contained in organic compost at least one year old can suppress such turfgrass diseases as dollarspot, brown patch, and gray snow mold

(Top) A tank sprayer is a useful tool for applying liquid lawn chemicals and water-soluble fertilizers.

(Left) Always wear a respirator when applying lawn pesticides and herbicides to avoid potential hazard from poisoning or allergic reactions.

and can mitigate pythium blight and necrotic ring-spot infections. Applying ¼ inch (6 mm) of this "suppressive" compost monthly, or at least in spring and autumn, may effectively ward off these diseases. In addition, some turfgrasses are disease resistant, and planting a mixed lawn of different but compatible turfgrass types can stem an onslaught that otherwise might infect an entire lawn.

Nature's weapons also include an arsenal against pest malefactors. Nematodes, microscopic worms that eat underground larvae of such lawn pests as Japanese beetles, mole crickets, sod webworm, and cutworms, are prime predators. You can buy nematodes at most nurseries and home garden centers in powdered form. Just mix it in water, pour over a moist lawn, and these critters will do the rest. The bacterium *Bacillus thuringiensis*, or BT, also attacks pest larvae but goes after butterfly and moth larvae as well, so use it sparingly.

Store garden chemicals safely and use protective gear for mixing and applying them, including waterproof gloves, eye protectors, and a respirator.

There also are so-called botanical insecticides that use environment-friendly compounds derived from plants. Neem, from the tropical tree *Azadirachta indica*, works on feeding insects, including aphids, and repels Japanese beetles. Pyrethrin, which comes from a daisy species, works on webworms and white grubs but also kills good bugs, so spot use it only. Insecticidal soaps, which are derived from fatty acids, kill soft-bodied pests and are non-toxic. Then, of course, there is plain old dish soap (not detergent), which many gardeners swear by to deter a host of pests. Mix it with water and spray over the lawn in spring and autumn.

Keep in mind that the foundation of IPM is that pests should be managed, not eradicated entirely. This philosophy means tolerating a certain amount of pests because the benefit to the micro- and macro-environment outweighs the price that must be paid. Whatever you decide, make sure that your choice is well considered.

Always follow all of the package-label instructions when selecting, mixing, applying, or disposing of garden chemicals.

U.S.D.A. Plant Hardiness Zones
of North America

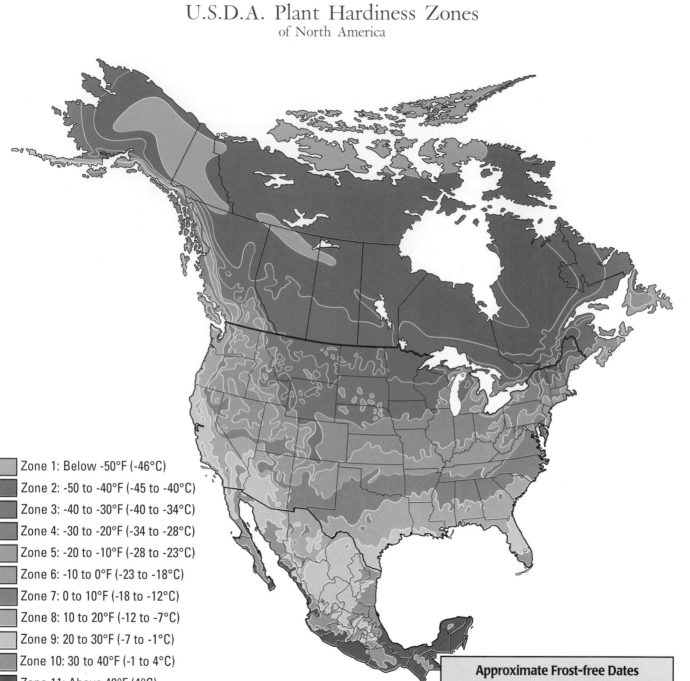

Zone 1: Below -50°F (-46°C)

Zone 2: -50 to -40°F (-45 to -40°C)

Zone 3: -40 to -30°F (-40 to -34°C)

Zone 4: -30 to -20°F (-34 to -28°C)

Zone 5: -20 to -10°F (-28 to -23°C)

Zone 6: -10 to 0°F (-23 to -18°C)

Zone 7: 0 to 10°F (-18 to -12°C)

Zone 8: 10 to 20°F (-12 to -7°C)

Zone 9: 20 to 30°F (-7 to -1°C)

Zone 10: 30 to 40°F (-1 to 4°C)

Zone 11: Above 40°F (4°C)

Approximate Frost-free Dates	
Zone 1	July 20–August 31
Zone 2	July 10–September 10
Zone 3	June 30 September 15
Zone 4	June 15–September 25
Zone 5	May 25–October 10
Zone 6	May 15–October 20
Zone 7	April 25–November 1
Zone 8	April 15–November 10
Zone 9	March 15–November 15
Zone 10	February 10–December 10
Zone 11	Frost-free All Year

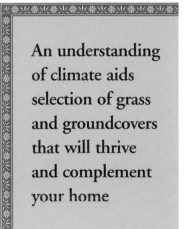

A lawn is not one plant but a colony of millions of individual plants. Grasses are monocotyledons, meaning they produce a single seed leaf, while all of the broad-leafed plants start out with two seed leaves.

All turfgrasses belong to the family *Gramineae*. Lawns usually are composed of perennial species of the grass genera *Agrostis* (bent grass), *Axonopus* (carpet grass), *Buchloe* (Buffalo grass), *Cynodon* (Bermuda grass), *Festuca* (fescue), *Lolium* (ryegrass), *Poa* (bluegrass), *Stenotaphrum* (St. Augustine grass), and *Zoysia* (zoysia). Other grass species include ornamentals, cereal, and other food grasses, forage grasses, and bamboos.

Some grasses—annual and perennial ryegrass, zoysia, and tall fescue among them—are bunch grasses, meaning they grow in tufts, sending out side shoots called tillers from the main crown of the rooted plant. Others, such as bent grass, Kentucky bluegrass, and Bermuda grass, are creepers, sending out horizontal runners called stolons and below-ground runners called rhizomes that root and create new plants.

Warm-season grasses are creepers, while cool-season grasses either bunch or creep. Some turfgrasses, particularly the warm-season grasses, are coarse textured, meaning their blades are wider than 1/4 inch (6 mm). Others, such as zoysia, the bent grasses, buffalo grass, and Kentucky bluegrass, are fine textured, with narrow blades 1/4 inch (6 mm) wide or less. The coarse grasses produce a rough-textured lawn while the fine grasses produce a more refined, even-textured lawn.

Most turfgrasses are perennial, meaning they grow and spread from year to year. Others, such as annual ryegrass, are annuals, meaning they complete the process of germination from seed, growth, flowering, seed production, and death within a season. Annual grasses are seldom used for lawns.

In the pages that follow, you will be introduced to outstanding turfgrasses and groundcovers, ideal for your home landscapes and lawn.

An understanding of climate aids selection of grass and groundcovers that will thrive and complement your home

Turfgrasses & Groundcovers

Find your plant hardiness zone on the U.S.D.A. scale by identifying your locale, noting its color, and comparing that color to the legend. Remember that local conditions— shade, slope of site, prevailing winds, or other factors—may cause your garden to vary from the surrounding area by a zone or more.

TURFGRASSES

Common name: Bahia Grass

Scientific name: *Paspalum notatum*

Description: A tough, coarse grass, introduced into the U.S. from Brazil. Light green with hairy blades. Slow to germinate but vigorous. Green throughout the year unless temperatures go below freezing. Bahia grass creeps with surface runners, which put out deep roots. Drought resistant. Best warm-season grass for shade tolerance. Mow 2–3 in. (5–8 cm) high.

Season: Warm season. Heaviest use in Southeastern U.S., from North Carolina to Florida, east to coastal Texas.

Plant hardiness: Zones 7–10.

Soil needs: Grows best in sandy, fairly infertile soil. An acid 5.0–6.5 pH soil is best. Fertilize in early spring, early summer, and late autumn at ½ lb. (225 g) nitrogen per 1,000 sq. ft. (93 m^2).

Sun requirement: Full sun; will tolerate shade.

Watering requirement: Water frequently, but will survive some drought.

Seed/turf/plug planting: Seed, turf.

Care and use: Bahia grass provides a low-upkeep home lawn. Its coarse texture makes mowing difficult. Considered a weed in fine lawns. Wear resistant. Pest trouble in the form of leaf hoppers and army worms; prone to brown patch and dollar spot.

Common name: Bent Grass, Creeping

Scientific name: *Agrostis palustris*

Description: The finest-textured and lowest-growing cool-season grass. Produces a high-quality, very high maintenance lawn. Spreads by aboveground stolons. Mow to ¼–½ in. (0.6–1.25 cm) Finest playing surface for golf, putting, and bowling greens, lawn tennis and croquet courts. Above ½ in. (1.25 cm), creeping bent grass develops thatch. Tolerates some heat.

Season: Cool season. Best regions are Northeast U.S. and coastal Pacific Northwest.

Plant hardiness: Zones 4–8.

Soil needs: Prefers moist, uncompacted, neutral 7.0 pH soil. Requires good drainage. Apply ¼–½ lb. (112–225 g) of nitrogen fertilizer per 1,000 sq. ft. (93 m^2) monthly during active growth.

Sun requirement: Full sun but will tolerate light shade.

Watering requirement: Frequent watering.

Seed/turf/plug planting: Seed.

Care and use: Requires constant care, in mowing and watering and the reduction of pests and fungus to which it is prone. Not the best choice for a home lawn unless you are establishing an area for a putting green or tennis lawn.

Common name: Bermuda Grass, Hybrid

Scientific name: *Cynodon*

Description: A softer, denser, more finely textured grass than common Bermuda. A bit more costly to grow as it is established by sod rather than seed. Grows into an elegant, green, drought-tolerant, heat-loving, well-wearing lawn for the money. Needs somewhat more fertilizer and mowing upkeep than common Bermuda grass. Mow ½–1 in. (1.25–2.5 cm) high.

Season: Warm season. A grass for the Southern U.S., Southeast, and Gulf, East, and mild-weather West coasts.

Plant hardiness: Zones 6–10.

Soil needs: Does well in acid to neutral 5.5–7.0 pH fertile soil. Apply ½–1 lb. (225–450 g) nitrogen per 1,000 sq. ft. (93 m²) each month during active growing period. Apply more if needed to boost appearance or repair wear damage.

Sun requirement: Full sun.

Watering requirement: Water regularly to keep at its best; it can tolerate some dryness.

Seed/turf/plug planting: Turf, plugs.

Care and use: Mow twice a week during active growth, especially in summer, otherwise lawn may yellow. Lawn will go dormant and turn brown in cold weather and over winter in mild climates. Very resistant to disease and pests. A top choice for high-visibility landscapes, golf courses, and home lawns with owners willing to tolerate its high maintenance requirements.

Common name: Bluegrass, Kentucky

Scientific name: *Poa pratensis*

Description: A moderate to fine-textured vigorous grass. The blades are boat shaped at the tips. It is blue-green in color and sets the standard as the most widely planted of the cool-season grasses. Tolerates cold very well but goes dormant during prolonged hot, dry weather. The sod that forms is strong and able to withstand punishment. Mow 1½–2½ in. (3.75–6.25 cm). Slow to germinate.

Season: Cool season. Northern U.S. and mountain areas and the cool regions of the South and Southwest do well with this grass.

Plant hardiness: Zones 2–7.

Soil needs: Rich, loamy, well-drained soil, pH range, 6.0–7.5. Apply ½–1 lb. (225–450 g) of nitrogen per 1,000 sq. ft. (93 m²) during growing period.

Sun requirement: Full sun; some varieties can tolerate shade.

Watering requirement: Water frequently; soil should not be constantly wet.

Seed/turf/plug planting: Seed.

Care and use: Many cultivars are available; it's best to blend several varieties to strengthen the disease and pest resistance of your lawn. Consult a local nursery to see which blend suits your area best. Many varieties are highly resistant to pests and diseases. Used for athletic fields, parks, and general-purpose turf. Historically, one of the earliest grasses used in America when the lawn became a common addition to the home.

Common name: Buffalo Grass

Scientific name: *Buchloe dactyloides*

Description: A native of arid sections of the Great Plains, Texas, and Arizona. Slow-growing, fine-bladed gray-green grass grows less than 5 in. (13 cm) high. Drought and heat tolerant. Not tolerant of humidity. Good cold resistance; dormant from September to May. Spreads by extending stolons and roots. Only 2–3 mowings a year. Mow ½–2½ in. (1.25–6.25 cm) high.

Season: Warm season. Plant where summers are dry.

Plant hardiness: Zones 4–8.

Soil needs: Rich, well-drained, clay soil is best. Avoid acid soil; 7.0–8.5 pH. Low to medium fertility; fertilize with 1–2 lb. (450–900 g) of nitrogen per 1,000 sq. ft. (93 m²).

Sun requirement: Full sun.

Watering requirement: Water well for several weeks to help seeds germinate. Water lightly once established.

Seed/turf/plug planting: Seed, plugs.

Care and use: The most lawnlike in appearance of all the native grasses. Pest and disease resistant; good wearability. Fine for low-maintenance grounds and lawns especially in drought-prone regions. Some use for golf course fairways and roughs.

Common name: Centipede Grass

Scientific name: *Eremochloa ophiuroides*

Description: A light-green, coarse, easy-maintenance grass whose thick, spreading stolons send out many roots. It's a slow-growing grass that never gets higher than 4–5 in. (10–15 cm). Susceptible to frost; becomes dormant in cold weather. Moderately drought resistant; does well in poor soil and requires less mowing than Bermuda grass. Mow 1–2 in. (2.5–5 cm) high. Affectionately known as the lazy man's grass.

Season: Warm season. Very popular in Florida and the Deep South. Also does well in other sections of Southeastern U.S., Gulf Coast, and Hawaii.

Plant hardiness: Zones 7–9.

Soil needs: Does best in a moist, sandy soil. Can take a more acidic soil than most grasses, down to 4.0–6.0 pH. Alkaline soil is not good as it leads to iron deficiencies. Fertilize in the spring and early autumn. Less than ¼ lb. (125 g) nitrogen per 1,000 sq. ft. (93 m²) during active growth. Low-fertility conditions are best.

Sun requirement: Full sun; tolerates some shade.

Watering requirement: Water frequently.

Seed/turf/plug planting: Seed, turf, plugs.

Care and use: Resistant to chinch bugs but problems with nematodes, leaf hoppers, and mole crickets. If planted by sea or ocean, salt spray can pose a threat. Best in areas where fertility is low and where use and care is minimal.

Common name: Fescue, Chewings

Scientific name: *Festuca rubra commutata*

Description: An aggressive fine fescue that can overrun other garden grasses. Forms a high-density, drought-tolerant lawn. Leaf blades are a needlelike folded sheath with pointed tips. Fairly drought tolerant, but intolerant of high temperatures. Maintenance needs are low. Mow 1–2 ½ in. (2.5–6.25 cm) high.

Season: Cool season. Works best under cool and humid conditions particularly in the northern U.S. and at higher elevations. The coastal regions of the Northeast and Pacific Northwest make good hosts too.

Plant hardiness: Zones 2–7.

Soil needs: Adapts well to sandy, well-drained, acidic 6.5 pH infertile soil. Do not overfertilize; 1–2 lb. (450–900 g) of nitrogen per 1,000 sq. ft. (300 m²) per year will serve the purpose.

Sun requirement: Excellent shade turf.

Watering requirement: Water infrequently; not a thirsty lawn.

Seed/turf/plug planting: Seed.

Care and use: Works well in shady low-traffic areas and lawns. This fine fescue is the most drought and shade tolerant of the cool-season grasses. Vulnerable to fungal diseases in periods of hot, wet weather. Crowds out weeds. May be ideal for dry, shady areas that are neglected.

Common name: Fescue, Creeping Red

Scientific name: *Festuca rubra rubra*

Description: Medium to dark green, finely textured, with needlelike folded blades. The lower sheaths are reddish in color. Often mixed with Kentucky bluegrass and others for a high-quality seed mix. It blends well and gives bluegrasses more shade tolerance. Also more wear and drought tolerant than chewings fescue. Grass height 3 in. (9 cm). Mow 1 ½–2 ½ in. (3.75–6.25 cm) high.

Season: Cool season. Adapts best to cool, humid areas. Coastal areas of the Northeast and Pacific Northwest are good as are higher elevations. The northern part of the U.S. is well suited.

Plant hardiness: Zones 2–7.

Soil needs: Tolerates poor and slightly acid to neutral soil, 6.5–7.0 pH. Don't overfertilize; 1–2 lb. (450–900 g) nitrogen per 1,000 sq. ft. (93 m²) per year.

Sun requirement: Excellent shade tolerance.

Watering requirement: Low to moderate watering.

Seed/turf/plug planting: Seed.

Care and use: Grows well on slopes and banks, but avoid wet sites. Very lush when left unmowed and natural. Best grass for shade. Slow to spread and easy to maintain. The less fertilizer used, the better. This grass will resist the fungus disease to which it is prone in hot weather. Its spreading qualities make it useful as a filler for gaps between stones. Used for parks and professional landscapes.

Common name: Fescue, Dwarf
Scientific name: *Festuca arundinacea*
Description: Newly developed dwarf cultivars lend more drought tolerance, wearability, and insect and disease resistance to the tall fescue family. The low growth of dwarf turf type also guarantees a lawn with fewer clippings of which to dispose after mowing to its 1–1½ in. (2.5–3.75 cm) height. Gives the appearance of Kentucky bluegrass but can tolerate the heat that bluegrass cannot. Finely textured, dark-green grass with a deep root system.
Season: Cool season. Does well in almost any climate except at high altitude. Better adapted to warmer areas of the U.S., such as the Southwest or Nevada, than tall fescue. Not winter hardy.
Plant hardiness: Zones 3–9.
Soil needs: Will tolerate many soil types, with pH ranges from quite acid to alkaline 5.5–7.5. Little fertilizer needed; ¼–½ lb. (112–225 g) nitrogen per 1,000 sq. ft. (93 m²) during growth period.
Sun requirement: Full sun to full shade.
Watering requirement: Infrequent watering.
Seed/turf/plug planting: Seed. Seed mix: tall fescue 60 percent/dwarf variety 40 percent.
Care and use: Dwarf turf type works well in home lawns and play areas. Its heat, drought, and shade tolerance and the elegance of its low-cut appearance make it a more flexible choice for areas where conventional fescues won't do. Varieties include Austin, Balexas, Bonsai, Marathon III, Phoenix, Tomahawk.

Common name: Fescue, Hard
Scientific name: *Festuca longifolia*
Description: A fine-textured, slow-growth bunch grass that grows into a high-density lawn, grayish to dark green in color. Growth is short and compact; leaf blades are needlelike and tough. A minimal-maintenance lawn that does well in dry, shaded areas. Mow 1½–2½ in. (3.75–6.25 cm) high.
Season: Cool season. Northern U.S. and high-elevation regions are well adapted. Cool coastal parts of the Northeast and Pacific Northwest are also good.
Plant hardiness: Zones 3–8.
Soil needs: Tolerates moist and dry soils. Slightly acidic to neutral 6.5–7.0 pH. Apply ¼–½ lb. (112–225 g) nitrogen per 1,000 sq. ft. (93 m²) during growth period. Do not overfertilize.
Sun requirement: Excellent shade grass.
Watering requirement: Water lightly, very drought tolerant.
Seed/turf/plug planting: Seed.
Care and use: Since hard fescue grows low and slow, mowing needs are few. It's a good turf for any low-maintenance areas, roadsides, or golf courses outside the rough. Probably the healthiest of all the fine fescues; resistant to leaf and dollar spot. Not particularly hard wearing; well suited to covering a bank or slope for soil stabilization. Mixes well with other grasses.

Common name: Fescue, Tall

Scientific name: *Festuca arundinacea*

Description: A leafy, coarse bunch grass with a vigorous, low growth habit. Medium to dark green; blades are broad and ribbed. Tolerant of a wide variety of conditions: poor soils, wet or dry sites, shade, heat, cold, and drought. A very durable, low-maintenance utility grass. Mow 1½–2 in. (3.75–5 cm) high for athletic use, otherwise mow 2–3 in. (5–8 cm) high.

Season: Cool season. Adapts best to northern U.S. and mountain regions, areas of the Southwest with mild winters and warm summers.

Plant hardiness: Zones 2–7.

Soil needs: Although a heavy soil is best, this grass tolerates many soil conditions as well as poor drainage; pH can range from acid to alkaline, 6.0–7.5. Apply ¼–½ lb. (112–225 g) nitrogen per 1,000 sq. ft. (93 m²) during growth period. Do not overfertilize as this may produce brown patches.

Sun requirement: Full sun to partial shade.

Watering requirement: Water infrequently but deeply.

Seed/turf/plug planting: Seed, turf.

Care and use: Not a good mix with other grasses but a superb turf for athletic fields, roadside planting, erosion control, in transition zones, and as a rugged home lawn. Tall fescue may thin out under very cold conditions. Tolerates high or infrequent mowing and is disease resistant.

Common name: Ryegrass, Annual

Scientific name: *Lolium multiflorum*

Description: A coarse grass that yields a lawn of moderate wear resistance. The lawn lives for only one year and grows vigorously in the winter and early spring. Fairly heat tolerant and does well under cold and dry conditions. Very quick to establish. Mow 1½–2 in. (3.75–5 cm) high.

Season: Cool season. Good in climates with mild winters and warm summers. The South, Northeast, and Pacific Northwest are compatible regions for this grass.

Plant hardiness: Zones 4–8.

Soil needs: Tolerates low pH, 6.0–7.0, acid to neutral soil. Also performs adequately in poorly drained, heavy soils. Apply ¼–½ lb. (112–225 g) nitrogen per 1,000 sq. ft. (93 m²) each month during active growth.

Sun requirement: Full sun; does not like shade.

Watering requirement: Moderate to frequent watering when conditions are dry. Not drought tolerant.

Seed/turf/plug planting: Seed.

Care and use: For use as a temporary, interim, or overseeded lawn. Since it germinates so quickly, it is often seeded over warm-season lawns that go dormant and turn unsightly brown from autumn to late spring, during cool, short days. Annual ryegrass keeps the landscape green under these off-season conditions, then dies quickly just at the point that the regular grass begins to awaken from dormancy. Rapid growth rate means frequent mowing. Also helpful for erosion control, wildlife cover, and in pastures.

Common name: Ryegrass, Perennial
Scientific name: *Lolium perenne*
Description: High-yield, quickly establishing grass. Bright-green bunch grass with a fine to medium texture. One of the most preferred grasses for dairy and sheep forage. Tolerates heavy foot traffic. Mow 1½–2 in. (3.75–5 cm) high. Not especially drought or cold tolerant. A low-maintenance lawn.
Season: Cool season. Best in cool, moist areas with mild winters, coastal areas of the Northeast, and temperate to cool sections of the Midwest and West.
Plant hardiness: Zones 3–7.
Soil needs: Neutral, 7.0. pH. Grows well in a heavy, moist soil, but you can add compost or other organic matter if the soil is sandy or a heavy clay. Apply ¼–½ lb. (112–225 g) nitrogen fertilizer per 1,000 sq. ft. (93 m^2) during active growth.
Sun requirement: Full sun; will tolerate slight shade.
Watering requirement: Water frequently.
Seed/turf/plug planting: Seed, turf.
Care and use: Perennial ryegrass has the best wear tolerance of any of the cool-season grasses. It is a natural for sporting fields and home lawns that receive a lot of traffic and play. Not at its best in shaded areas or in extremes of cold and hot. Resistant to pests and diseases. Good erosion-control grass.

Common name: St. Augustine Grass
Scientific name: *Stenotaphrum secundatum*
Description: Forms an attractive, very dense, very weed-proof lawn. Low-growing and coarse leaves are blue-green. Wears well. Not cold resistant and turns brown in winter. Is the most shade tolerant of all the warm season grasses. Mow 1½–2 in. (3.75–5 cm) high.
Season: Warm season. Particularly suited to the deep South on into Florida, the Gulf Coast states, and Southern California.
Plant hardiness: Zones 8–10.
Soil needs: A moist, sandy, well-drained soil is best; pH ranges from 6.0–7.0 are good. Fertilize in early spring, early summer, and late autumn; ½–1 lb. (225–450 g) of nitrogen per 1,000 sq. ft. (93 m^2) during active growing periods.
Sun requirement: Full sun; will tolerate full shade.
Watering requirement: Water frequently.
Seed/turf/plug planting: Seed, turf, or plug.
Care and use: Susceptible to fungus, chinch bugs, army worms, sod webworms, nematodes, and a viral disease known as St. Augustine Decline (SAD), which weakens and yellows the turf. Handles salt spray and heat. Provides a thick turf for shaded landscapes.

Common name: Zoysia

Scientific name: *Zoysia*

Description: A dense and wiry turfgrass that is wear tolerant but tough to mow given its needlelike blades and generally coarse texture. Tolerant of heat and drought, it gives one of the most uniform appearances of all the warm-season grasses. It also goes dormant in the cold sooner than many other species, staying brown from September up to late May. Slow growing, it spreads by means of underground rhizomes and aboveground stolons. Mow 1–2 in. (2.5–5 cm) high.

Season: Warm season. At its best in the coastal areas of the South and Southern California.

Plant hardiness: Zones 6–9.

Soil needs: Does well in most any type of soil , as long as it is well drained. Range, slightly acid to mildly alkaline, 6.0–7.5 pH. Fertilize with ¼–½ lb. (112–225 g) nitrogen per 1,000 sq. ft. (93 m²) during active growing months.

Sun requirement: Full sun; will tolerate some shade.

Watering requirement: Low watering requirements.

Seed/turf/plug planting: Turf, plug.

Care and use: Pest and disease resistant but fairly high maintenance given its mowing and de-thatching needs. Slow growing. Good for use in home-lawn transition areas. Good play surface.

GROUNDCOVERS

Common name: Bellflower, Serbian

Scientific name: *Campanula poscharskyana*

Description: This drought-resistant perennial groundcover grows in a loose, tumbling manner. Spreads rapidly by runners and blooms with a profusion of star-shaped, 1-in. (2.5-cm) purple flowers in the spring to early summer. Makes a spectacular color display. Leaves are 1½ in. (3.75 cm) wide and heart-shaped. Grows to 6 in. (15 cm) high. Dies down to the ground in winter.

Plant hardiness: Zones 3–10.

Soil needs: Average, dry-to-moist, well-drained soil. Moderate fertility. Neutral 7.0 pH.

Sun requirement: Full sun is fine in cooler climes, but in the hotter zones 8–10, partial shade is recommended.

Watering requirement: Low to moderate watering.

Planting methods and spacing: Divide plants in spring or autumn and plant at those times, or take stem cuttings in the summer and plant them in early autumn. Can also plant by seed. Space 10–12 in. (25–30 cm) apart.

Tips and use: Low-maintenance and foot-traffic-hardy plant. Works well in seashore locations. Used for borders, rock gardens, low edging, and containers. Should be cut back after flowering to curb fairly aggressive growth.

Common name: Bugleweed, Carpet

Scientific name: *Ajuga reptans*

Description: A creeping perennial that grows in 4–6-in. (10–15-cm) mounds and stays evergreen in mild climates. Forms a dense mat of small oval leaves; slender stalks bloom with clusters of tiny blue flowers in the spring and early summer. Deep-green foliage turns a reddish bronze in autumn. Spreads rapidly by runners. Carpet bugleweed was bought to the U.S. by colonists who prized its medicinal properties. It is primarily found throughout the Eastern seaboard and still makes a decent cup of tea. Member of the mint family.

Plant hardiness: Zones 4–9.

Soil needs: Does well in a wide range of soils, sandy, loamy, or clay; but rich, moist, well-drained conditions are best. Fertility can be average to moderate. Acid to neutral 6.0–7.0 pH.

Sun requirement: Full sun is fine but performs excellently in partial to deeply shaded areas.

Watering requirement: Water moderately.

Planting methods and spacing: Divide young plants from the parent plant after first spring growth. Plant in spring. Space plants 6–12 in. (15–30 cm) apart.

Tips and use: Low-maintenance groundcover that is dense enough to choke out weeds and prevent soil erosion. May be invasive and harmful to other plants if placed in a rock garden, where it commonly has been used. Nice as a border for an edged path. Apply fungicide if crown rot becomes a problem.

Common name: Cinquefoil, Spring

Scientific name: *Potentilla tabernaemontani*

Description: One of the big family of cinquefoils—evergreen perennials that combine many foliage and flower characteristics of the rose and strawberry. It is a dense, drought-resistant, low-growing groundcover that does very well in the Rocky Mountain states, the Great Plains, and the Southwest. Long, slender stems creep along the ground and take root as they go. Yellow flowers are saucer-shaped and bloom from spring into early autumn. Green, fingerlike leaflets form mats that grow 3–6 in. (7.5–15 cm) high. Mow annually to renew growth from roots.

Plant hardiness: Zones 5–9.

Soil needs: Moist, humus-rich, well-drained soil works well. A range of acid to neutral 6.5–7.0 pH is best. Fertility moderate, but tolerates infertile soils.

Sun requirement: Full sun to partial shade.

Watering requirement: Low to moderate water needs.

Planting methods and spacing: Grow from seed in the spring or propagate by cuttings of fresh shoots. Space plants 10 in. (25 cm) apart.

Tips and use: Excellent in rock gardens or to protect soil from erosion. A low-maintenance groundcover that works well over large areas. Tolerates some foot traffic. Attracts butterflies.

Common name: Hens and Chickens

Scientific name: *Sempervivum tectorum*

Description: A low, mounded, succulent perennial with thick, fleshy leaves and bristly white hairs. Grows in rosettes 2–4 in. (5–10 cm) across, surrounded by a circular array of smaller rosettes. A 9-in. (23-cm) spike rises from a mature 6-in. (15-cm) to 1-ft. (30-cm) rosette and blooms in summer with a reddish-purple flower. Very drought and heat tolerant; excellent xeriscape planting.

Plant hardiness: Zones 5–10. Not a good planting for humid Gulf Coast states where fungal diseases are a problem.

Soil needs: Well-drained, ordinary garden soil. No fertilizer is necessary and may cause abnormal growth. Neutral 7.0 pH.

Sun requirement: Full sun.

Watering requirement: Minimal watering.

Planting methods and spacing: Easily planted from cuttings any time of the year. Space plants 6–9 in. (15–23 cm) apart. Can also plant from seed.

Tips and uses: A quickly spreading groundcover, but also popular in rock gardens, containers, and for borders. Works very nicely in a miniature garden. Hens and chickens was used as an old home remedy to cure warts, and the malic acid contained within the leaves has been proven to shrink tissue. It was also planted on rooftops to ward off thunder and lightning—no science currently supports that efficacy.

Common name: Lantana, Trailing

Scientific name: *Lantana montevidensis*

Description: A low growing, rambling, perennial evergreen that bursts with color in the summer as dainty, 1-in. (2.5-cm) lavender flowers start to bloom. Used mostly in southern or warmer climes throughout the U.S. as a groundcover, due to its poor tolerance of freezing temperatures. The thick mass of foliage spreads and roots rapidly. Leaves have a pungent odor. Tolerates heat and drought, and beach and salty conditions.

Plant hardiness: Zones 8–11.

Soil needs: Light, well-drained, moist soil. Will tolerate poor soil but best to enrich with compost and keep moderately fertile to encourage flowering. Will also tolerate dry soil, but if you can keep it moist, it won't hurt. Neutral 7.0 pH.

Sun requirement: Full sun.

Watering requirement: Moderate watering.

Planting methods and spacing: Can start from seed, but grows more quickly from stem cuttings. Plant in the spring; place plants 18 in. (45 cm) apart.

Tips and use: Trailing lantana can be staked and will rise 18–24 in. (45–60 cm). To eliminate old, woody stems, cut the plants back in spring before new growth starts. Trim and prune lightly after flowers drop. Commonly used in hanging containers, especially in colder parts of the country where it will not overwinter unless protected indoors. Also popularly used for edging, borders, erosion control, and bank cover. Attracts butterflies.

Common name: Mock Strawberry, Indian

Scientific name: *Duchensnea indica*

Description: A dark-green perennial with 1–3 in. (2.5–7.5 cm) leaves. The three-leaved plant resembles wild strawberry, but ¾-in. (1.8-cm) flowers are yellow instead of white. Decorative 1-in. (2.5-cm) red berries are edible but unpalatable. 2–6-in.-high (5–15-cm) mats are quickly spread by runners. Retains color into the winter. Drought tolerant.

Plant hardiness: Zones 4–9. Found across the country in many environments, from desert to sea.

Soil needs: Average, well-drained soil is best. Acid to neutral 6.5–7.0 pH. Low fertility and maintenance needs.

Sun requirement: Some sun is all right, but this is an excellent plant for partial to fully shaded areas.

Watering requirement: Water moderately.

Planting methods and spacing: From seed or sprigs of old plants. Space plants 12–18 in. (30–45 cm) apart; plant in spring.

Tips and uses: Mock strawberry is hardy but tolerates only occasional foot traffic. Use it for hedging, hanging baskets, and containers. Vulnerable to invasion by weeds but is itself considered a weed when it encroaches onto turfgrass.

Common name: Mondo Grass

Scientific name: *Ophiopogon japonicus*

Description: A fine-textured, turflike perennial groundcover with glossy dark-green foliage. Grows to an average of 6 in. (15 cm) high; clump forming. Small lavender flowers appear in summer followed by ½-in. (13-mm) blue berries. Member of the lily family. An outstanding groundcover for shade conditions; grows well even under trees and shrubs. Has tough roots that are spread by underground stems. Drought, heat, and salt-spray resistant.

Plant hardiness: Zones 7–11. A good groundcover for warm climates.

Soil needs: Rich, moist, well-drained soil is best, but does well in most soils. Average to rich fertility. Acidic to neutral 6.5–7.0 pH.

Sun requirement: Partial sun is fine, but mondo grass does best in densely shaded areas.

Watering requirement: Water regularly.

Planting methods and spacing: Divide for propagation; easy to grow. Space plants 6–12 in. (15–30 cm) apart.

Tips and use: Used for edging, erosion control, and around shaded pool areas. Nice as a border, but make sure it doesn't become invasive. Seldom needs weeding, and no mowing is required. Shear to 1 in (2.5 cm) in the early spring before new growth appears. Spreads quickly and stays green all year in mild climates.

Common name: Moss, Irish

Scientific name: *Sagina subulata*

Description: An evergreen groundcover that forms dense, puffy cushions of brilliant green moss. Spiky ¼-in. (.6-cm) leaves are covered by ½–¾-in. (1.3–1.8-cm) white flowers that bloom in midsummer. Rapidly spread by thick creeping stems that hug the soil and roots as they go. Prefers a cool environment, not hot and dry conditions. Easy to grow, low maintenance, and very attractive. Perfect for container gardens, especially bonsai landscapes. Also known as Scotch moss.

Plant hardiness: Zones 4–9.

Soil needs: Soil should be dry to moist, well drained, and organically rich. Keep soil fertile with occasional feedings. Neutral 7.0 pH is fine.

Sun requirement: Full sun to full shade.

Watering requirement: Keep soil moist but always well drained.

Planting methods and spacing: Plant in the spring. Space plants 6 in. (15 cm) apart. New plants can be propagated by division after first flowering in the spring.

Tips and use: Hardy and tolerates foot traffic but can fall prey to snails, cutworms, and slugs. Well suited to rock gardens and for filling in crevices. Do not plant Irish moss near turfgrass or in flower beds—it will invade them easily.

Common name: Plantain Lily, Fragrant

Scientific name: *Hosta plantaginea*

Description: Lush foliage perfumed by very fragrant white flowers characterizes plantain lily. The leaves of this perennial are bright and glossy, greenish-yellow, and 6 in. (15 cm) wide. Grows in mounds to about 18 in. (45 cm). The flowers rise above the foliage on 2-ft. (60-cm) stalks and bloom in the late summer through early autumn. A heat-tolerant species of hosta but does very well in partial shade.

Plant hardiness: Zones 3–9.

Soil needs: Moist, rich, well-drained soil is ideal, but will tolerate a wide range of soils. Fertilize and enrich the soil with peat moss or leaf mold; feed regularly with balanced fertilizers in the growing season. Neutral 7.0 pH.

Sun requirement: Full sun is fine but partial shade is best.

Watering requirement: Water regularly; keep soil moist.

Planting methods and spacing: Grow by seed or plant by division. Divide clumps in early spring. Space plants 18 in. (45 cm) apart. Can also plant in the autumn.

Tips and use: Protect plantings with mulch for the first winter until established. Plantain lily makes an excellent groundcover but also is popular for beds, borders, fragrant flower cuttings, and container plants. Attracts hummingbirds. Guard against snails and slugs. Most of the 200 varieties of hosta have been developed by Japanese horticulturists where the plant is native and widely used, though the plant now has an international following and is widely cultivated.

Common name: Rosemary, Dwarf

Scientific name: *Rosmarinus officinalis prostratus*

Description: A low-growing, perennial, evergreen shrub. The glossy needlelike leaves are ½–2 in. (1.3–5 cm) long. They're dark green on top with an accent of white underneath. The leaves are aromatic. Tiny violet-blue flowers are aromatic as well and bloom midwinter to early spring. Diameter of the dwarf species reaches about 5–6 ft. (1.5–1.8 m), but good coverage may take a few years with this slow-to-spread plant. Excellent groundcover for hot and dry regions.

Plant hardiness: Zones 8–10.

Soil needs: Dry to moist, well-drained soil. Fertilize every 2–3 months but don't overdo it as this can make the plant woody. Neutral 7.0 pH.

Sun requirement: Full sun.

Watering requirement: Needs regular watering to establish. Once established, let the soil dry out between good waterings.

Planting methods and spacing: Stem cuttings are best. Space plants 18–24 in. (45–60 cm) apart. Can start from seed, but it is a slow process.

Tips and use: Used as a low border, container plant, and is easily pruned for more formal garden settings. Prevents soil erosion and works well in seaside conditions. Plant with an eye to good air circulation to prevent powdery mildew from forming. Watch out for spider mites and aphids. Attracts bees. You can keep dwarf rosemary stunted (under 15 in. [38 cm]) by pinching off the tips of stems; use as a cooking herb.

Common name: Sedum, Creeping

Scientific name: *Sedum kamtschaticum*

Description: Produces a ground-hugging carpet of thick, scallop-shaped leaves sporting star-shaped yellow flowers. An evergreen perennial also known as yellow or orange stonecrop. The light-green succulent leaves cascade beautifully and are ideal for the rock or xeriscape garden. Plant grows 1–2 ft. (30–60 cm) wide and 5–12 in. (13–30 cm) high. Flowers bloom July to autumn. Low maintenance and frost hardy.

Plant hardiness: Zones 4–10.

Soil needs: Sandy, well-drained soil. Average fertility. Acid to neutral 6.5–7.0 pH.

Sun requirement: Full sun; will tolerate light shade.

Watering requirement: Low to moderate watering needs.

Planting methods and spacing: Plant by seeds, division, or stem cuttings.

Tips and use: Not foot hardy; leaves crush easily. Deer-resistant planting. Very attractive growing next to a stone wall or for use in a border. Native to Japan, where it is popular as a landscaping plant.

Common name: Spurge, Japanese
Scientific name: *Pachysandra terminalis*
Description: One of the most popular evergreen groundcovers in the U.S. A hardy perennial that forms a rich carpet of foliage 8–12 in. (20–30 cm) tall. Dark-green, glossy, oval leaves 1–3 in. (2.5–7.5 cm) wide, are joined by 23 in. (58 cm) spikes of greenish-white flowers in the spring. A popular planting around tree bases as Japanese spurge does very well in shade. Established by creeping underground stems; growth is moderately slow.
Plant hardiness: Zones 4–9. Does not do well in regions with high heat and humidity.
Soil needs: Rich, moist, well-drained soil is best. Fertilize periodically with peat moss or leaf mold especially if plantings are in competition with tree roots. Acid to neutral 6.5–7.0 pH.
Sun requirement: Partial to full shade.
Watering requirement: Water moderately.
Planting methods and spacing: Propagate by dividing clumps or planting rooted stem cuttings. Plant in spring or early summer. Space plants 6–12 in. (15–30 cm) apart.
Tips and use: Mulch the soil with oak leaves or wood chips to help conserve moisture, but this is a fairly low-maintenance groundcover. Do check, however, on whether it is spreading beyond its borders; can be invasive, but thinning will help. Does not tolerate foot traffic. Is resistant to deer. Used in Japanese gardens as textural contrast to delicate mosses or grasses. Excellent for shady green borders, slopes, and banks.

Common name: Thyme, Creeping
Scientific name: *Thymus serpyllum*
Description: A trailing, perennial, very aromatic, evergreen herb. Also known wild thyme. Bright-green, tiny, round ¼-in. (6-mm) leaves form a flat, dense mat of groundcover that grows 16 in. (40 cm) high. In the summer, flower stalks sport purple, white, pink, red, or lavender blossoms. Rapidly spreading stems hug the soil as they go.
Plant hardiness: Zones 3-10. A native of North Africa, Europe, and Asia that has naturalized in the U.S.
Soil needs: Sandy, light, dry, well-drained soil is best with acid to alkaline 6.5–7.5 pH. Do not overfertilize as this can cause the stems of the groundcover to get tall and weak.
Sun requirement: Full sun; partial shade is fine.
Watering requirement: Water sparingly.
Planting methods and spacing: Can plant from seed, but easy to start from cuttings or divisions of old plants. Set plants 6–12 in. (15–30 cm) apart.
Tips and use: In areas of high humidity fungus diseases may damage or kill plants. Very attractive to bees. Popular for use in rock gardens although it may overrun the rocks and must be cut back. Add spice as a kitchen herb; some alternative medicine practitioners use it for bronchial conditions.

ON-LINE

INDEX

INDEX

INDEX